EQUIDO

Morag Higgins
&
Mark Higgins

Equido
Published by
Fisher King Publishing
The Studio
Arthington Lane
Pool-in-Wharfedale
LS21 1JZ
England

ISBN 978-1-906377-42-7

Cover design by
Samantha Richardson

From the authors...

To Morag, my wife, horse trainer,
Sensei and boss!

To my Family for all their support.

To my Aikido Sensei's; Don, Davy
and the rest of the crew - Arigato
Gozaimasu.

To all my friends.

And finally, a special dedication to
Ninjutsu Sensei Iain Colquhoun "A
fallen warrior, forever in our hearts and
memories".

Mark Higgins

You will not find any fancy techniques or
gadgets in this book, this is not about teaching
you things you can do to your horse, instead, it
will teach you how to be with your horse, how
to understand them and how to make their lives
better by improving yourself and your way of
thinking. All of the Equido work was inspired
by Mark Rashid and his unique ethos and I
would like to thank him personally for helping
us make this world a better place for the horse.

Morag Higgins

Contents

Introduction

If you've had horses in your life for any length of time, you probably have a few stories. Like most of ours, some are funny, some are touching and some are sad. What you will find in Equido Horsemanship for the 21st Century is just that, a way of thinking told from a point of view that is both compassionate and at the same time practical. What you will find here is not only a good book but also the wisdom learned and lessons horses teach us about them, life and also ourselves if we but choose to see.

Morag and Mark Higgins have been friends of ours for several years. They both practice the martial art of Ninjitsu and Aikido, respectively, and are two of the funniest and fun loving people we know. Their book contains much of their own unique brand of humour, and even amongst the times when the stories are emotionally provocative, the heart they have for their life and especially the horses under their care shines through. We also have the beautiful offerings of poetry from Mark that give us a glimpse into his deep connection to horses and all the gifts they give. (His poem "Home" is one of our personal favourites).

While Morag imparts knowledge in a way that owners will benefit from in their own horse care and management, she also addresses topics that she finds important to pass along. She is honest and forthright in her telling, and we have no doubt that she is an advocate for the horse. Her teachings on animal communication and horse awareness will open the readers mind and allow them to look at things from a different perspective.

What a gift it is to have such open access to the beauty, wisdom, kindness and knowledge that Morag and Mark share with us in Equido Horsemanship for the 21st Century. We are sure you will enjoy and treasure it just as much as we have.

Mark Rashid & Crissi McDonald
Estes Park, Colorado, U.S.A.

1

Chapter 1
Horsemanship for the 21st Century

Our relationship with the horse changed throughout the ages with each era bringing with it new ideas and revelations. This changing relationship has not always had the horses' best interests at heart and more often than not they found themselves getting the worst of the deal.

It may surprise you to learn that today there are more horses in the U.K. than there were before the Industrial Revolution, when the only "horsepower" was quite literally equipped with four legs. Now most people keep horses through choice rather than necessity and it should therefore follow that at last the human/horse partnership has a chance of growing into something quite special.

This book is an introduction of sorts into the world of Equido. Equido is more than an equestrian qualification, it is an ethos, a way of thinking and interacting with your horse that should enable you to step into a world of possibilities that you did not even know existed. Equido strives to show you a knew way, fit for this new century, of looking at all manner of horsemanship, from stable management, training, competing and rehabilitation, all from the horses' point of view because it is only when we look at things through their eyes that we can truly understand what it means to be a horse and understanding is the first step in communication.

You may have seen or heard about great horsemen and women and how they seemed to have a natural empathy or feel for a horse. They seemed able to almost "think" with their horses till the line between human and equine became blurred. You may (like most people) have wondered what this illusive feel actually was, what it meant to the rider and the horse and how it impacted on they way they work together. Many of you may even have been inspired by these horsemen to take your first tentative steps into the world of horses.

As you began to learn about the art of horsemanship and riding you may even have asked various instructors what feel was and may have received a multitude of different answers making the mystery of this empathy all the more intangible. How could something so obvious in some people be so difficult to understand and teach? The truth of the matter is that it is not difficult to learn or teach if you know how. Equido was developed to do just that. I have been riding now for over 37yrs and teaching for 30 of those years. I have had the privilege to have known and worked with many, many horses in my career and although I have always felt that they was something new to learn from every horse, it was only recently that I found a path to follow where I could for once truly listen to what they were saying.

I have had a very varied riding career, having participated in several disciplines such as jumping, dressage, one day eventing, showing and now western riding. I look back at the horses I have known and feel humble to have been taught by them.

I had a very traditional training and was myself a very traditional trainer and rider. This held me in good stead for the years of competition in strict disciplines, but through it all I felt I was always seeking more.

One day I saw a QED program about a Cowboy called Monty Roberts. I was amazed by what I saw. I immediately contacted his organisation and asked where I could learn his methods. He immediately put me in touch with Kelly Marks and the Intelligent Horsemanship Association and so I started on the journey of Natural Horsemanship. I began my studies with the Intelligent Horsemanship Association in 1999 and qualified two years later becoming the first person in Scotland to do so. I was made the Recommended Associate for Scotland in 2002 and continued in this role for four years.

Over the years I learned so much from the troubled horses I was working with and I began to build on and expand the techniques I had been shown. The moment of real revelation came when I had the really good fortune to ride on a clinic with top American trainer Mr Mark Rashid in 2005. I was truly inspired. Mark Rashid is not only an exceptional horseman but human being as well. A fellow Martial Artist, I instantly understood his ethos and he has been the real inspiration that has guided me down the path leading to the development of the Equido Training system.

At times I had to let go of previous beliefs and open my mind to new, and what seemed like, radical ideas.

I can honestly say that my training experience with Mr Mark Rashid has changed my life and changed me as a person. I have become a much better rider, more receptive and responsive to the horses I ride. I can now listen to what they are saying and feel how to correct any issues they may have. It was a revelation to me that riding could be taken to such a level where you only need think "half pass" and your horse would carry out your command with freedom and ease. No spurs, no double bridle, no whips, no aids, just pure co-operation and willingness from the horse to please and a meeting of minds.

Feel isn't about any one thing, it isn't a button you can press or a technique you can learn or a gadget or tack you can put on the horse to make him work "better". Feel is about listening instead of talking, clearing your mind and living in the moment, visualisation, breathing, and application of aids, timing and responsibility. Feel is a way of living and working in harmony with, not against nature.

This way of living influences every single thing we do with our horses, right from the moment we step into their world, be it mucking out, making feeds, leading, grooming, rugging etc, it is not just about when we sit on their backs and expect them to obey. Equido teaches you how do have feel for everything you do with the horse, it is about the big picture, the whole picture. We know that a horse that is not cared for or handled properly will not be in a good or happy state of mind and this in turn will affect their performance when being ridden.

I often ask my Equido students about the difference between their riding and a top Grand Prix dressage rider. Some laugh and start to list a whole series of "things" that make them think they are inferior riders to the top dressage elite. They are often taken aback when I simply say that there is no difference between them and a top rider other than their timing and the application of their aids. The one thing that separates most riders from the top echelons is this illusive feel. A really good rider will have trained themselves to "listen" to their horses, to "feel" what they are thinking and anticipate any questions the horse may be asking and correct them in the blink of an eye. A Grand Prix horse may be spooky or fresh and may want to shy away from the pretty flowers round the ring or throw in a buck out of sheer enjoyment. A Grand Prix rider will be able to "feel" this excitement and tension in their horse or the anxiety they may have and will be able to override these emotions with calm and focus sent down through their seat and reins and expertly applied aids to correct any potential deviation from their tests. The overall picture is one of complete harmony as the horse seems to do the test themselves and the rider is along for the fun of it. This is the mark of a good rider, someone who makes it all look easy, don't be fooled though, they will be working very hard to achieve this and their efforts will go largely unnoticed.

Through these pages we hope to give you an insight into what Equido is all about and what this qualification can help you achieve. We hope you will find our ethos interesting and entertaining and we will try to give you a taste of what it is we teach.

Once you start to ride this way you will be amazed at how much communication there actually is between you and the horse and how often he will ask you questions. Sometimes it is simply "have I to keep moving at this pace?" as you will "feel" a slight hesitation in his step, you can then apply a soft aid to say either "yes" or "no". Because your aids will become lighter and more subtle your horse will become more intent and will concentrate on what is going on, in other words he will start to "listen" to you. You may have heard instructors shout "make him listen!" and you may have seen an explosion of aids and flustering coming from the rider and the horse may start flustering right back! Perhaps the better expression would have been "ask him to listen!" this would give the rider the chance to think through what they need to do and the best way to encourage anyone (even the horse) to listen more intently is to whisper rather than shout!

Equido will hopefully allow both horse and rider start to listen to each other and they will be well on the way to achieving "feel". As time progresses the rider will be responding so quickly to their horse that it will almost become instinctive, they will no longer consciously think about applying a command, their body will do this automatically and the rider will start to "think" and "visualise" where they want to go and how their horse can carry out a manoeuvre. It will all begin to flow into one seamless stream of movement and dynamics as rider and horse become united in mind and purpose. This is feel, this is Equido. The ability to find and connect through the unspoken bond that can exist between man and horse. This bond is fragile and delicate, it is soft and translucent, it is almost intangible but the rewards are infinite.

Chapter Two
Where do we begin?

Equido is about teaching you how to understand your horse's needs in everything you do. This understanding will allow you to see much more clearly into his world and allow you to find a common ground on which to meet and work.

So what do horses' think about this world? Picture this:-There you are, wandering along, not a care in the world, at peace with yourself and your horse. The reins are at the buckle the birds are singing and your faithful steed is strolling along thinking about what might be for dinner. In an instant you find yourself seeming to levitate through the air sideways (usually around 15ft but feels like 50ft!) hopefully with the aforementioned faithful steed still underneath you but more often than not your steed will have continued on the levitation theme for a further 10ft leaving you hovering in mid air for a split second before crashing to the ground. There you lay, the wind knocked out of you, your heart making a frantic attempt to escape through your ribcage and bruises beginning to congregate in places you didn't think possible. As you either watch your now not so faithful steed leg it home or gaze upwards into two large concerned equine eyes examining you carefully, you wonder what the hell happened. Then, the cause of the mayhem becomes apparent, the most vicious, most dangerous of all predators known to man or horse, the white plastic bag emerges from its hiding place in the hedge and slowly wafts across the road and into the next field. You have just discovered that you have in fact been riding a giant timid rabbit.

It is seemingly illogical and erratic behaviour such as this that makes us wonder if horses have anything between their ears other than vacant air space and this is one of the main routes to total misunderstanding between our species. To us it is blatantly obvious that white plastic bags (one of the many strange and unusual predators of the horse today) are really no threat at all, but more often than not our horses think otherwise. So why does this intelligent and sentient species behave so stupidly at times? Equido can show you the answer, it all lies in their past.

It is common knowledge that horses evolved from small ancestors not much bigger than a fox and throughout their evolution and development they have found themselves predated upon by a variety of different species. The horse in the wild has certain needs or goals that he or she must satisfy and certain rules of behaviour that have been governed by inherited memory (genetic memory) and learned responses which allows them to fulfil these needs.

So, what does the wild horse want to achieve in life?

Have enough to eat to grow big, strong and fast.

Horses are pretty much governed by their appetite and this has evolved pretty much because of the main food they eat, grass. In order to get sufficient nutrition from their food source, they have to eat large quantities daily and this means they spend a lot of time eating (up to 2.5% of their own bodyweight a day). It is vital for the horse to eat enough not only to maintain good health but to develop strength for speed and defence. A strong fast horse that is fit and healthy is not an easy target for a predator and horses have a very "selfish" drive to get all the best food for themselves. It is very rare for two horses to share equally a good food source (it does happen between very close companions or mother and foal). I know that in our world there are no predators to hunt them, but remember, the horse has evolved over millions of years and has only been domesticated for a few thousand years. This genetic programming is just as strong in our domestic horses as it was when they were wild.

Have friends who will socialise with you.

Friendship is very important in the equine world and horses who do not have the opportunity to have other equine  friends will strike up a relationship with another animal species i.e. cats, dogs, sheep, goats etc. So why does the horse really need a friend? We all need to spend time in the company of those who understand us and no one understands a horse more than another horse. Animals of the same species speak the same language so there is no time lost in communicating an alert of potential predators etc. Friends can help defend each other and you are more likely to help a friend than a stranger, so being a good friend might just save your life one day. The other side of the coin is simple safety in numbers. If you have, for example, five friends with you, you have a one in five chance of being picked off by a predator, a single horse does not have such good odds.

Explore your surroundings.

In the wild horses have a large territory of several hundred square miles. Throughout this territory there are good places to eat, good places to drink, dangerous places to go, safe places to rest etc. In order to learn where to go (and where not to go!) it is very important that the horse explores his territory building up a mental map of where he has been. Nature has provided the horse with an almost photographic memory (even better than elephants!) and their ability to notice finite details in their surroundings is uncanny. This

ability stands them in good stead for spotting things that have changed or are out of place (like the new boulder by the side of the trail that wasn't there the day before and which might well be a predator lying in wait). A horse with a good map of their territory has a good chance of escaping and surviving in the wild and this drive to explore is still very strong even in our domestic horses (just see what happens if you leave a gate open!). They will repeatedly explore and wander round every area of their field and this behaviour can become stereotypical in the form of some vices which we will cover later.

Find a mate and reproduce.

This is one of the main drives for wild horses, continuation of the species. Growing up in a wild herd allows the horse to

express themselves fully and there are only two sexes, mares and stallions. A young horse will learn from watching the older horses mate and young males hone their fighting skills in bachelor groups before winning mares for themselves. Young female horses will flirt and run off with potential suitors, often joining new bands and so improving the gene pool, it is virtually unheard of for a stallion to mate with his own offspring and there is now evidence that some stallions will keep their daughters within their group but allow them to mate with stallions from other bands. We are only just beginning to touch on the complexities of equine family life in the wild and it is blowing some previously held beliefs right out of the water.

In domestication we have created a third sex, the gelding. Most geldings behave like adolescent males who are not fully sexually mature, or like stallions who are not in the "breeding" cycle. As such they can live quite happily with mares or other geldings without any conflict. Mares on the other hand are, like stallions, "entire" and so will go through the drive every year to seek out a mate and reproduce. This seems to annoy some human owners who blame the horse for being difficult, or moody, or nasty, when, in truth, they are simply being horses. In some yards mares and geldings are separated and this can lead to some serious problems, would you for example, keep a herd of stallions next to a field of mares with only a small fence separating them? Yet we keep "entire" mares next to fields of geldings and expect the mares not to be driven to seek out male company.

Stay alive. In order to achieve any of the other needs it is vital that the horse stays alive. All of their super keen senses and ability for self preservation is geared towards this. In order to stay alive the horse must be pretty sure about what to do about predators. Nature has successfully programmed the horse throughout the millennia to recognise certain dangerous shapes. It is inbuilt into their psyche that certain body shapes, movement's even colours can indicate the presence of a predator. The basic body shapes that are imprinted into their minds are:-

The bear. Any large moving object that resembles this outline must be treated with caution. Small cars can be very bear like in appearance.

The wolf. This will include all animals such as dogs or even some types of sheep!

The bird of prey. This goes back to the time when horses were small enough to be eaten by such birds. This makes them highly suspicious of anything moving or flapping over their heads or backs.

The big cat. The flight response can be triggered by the stereotypical way that big cats prowl, stalk and hunt. Therefore any creeping, slinking, low slung shape or movement must be treated with suspicion. Often cyclists mimic the movement of a fast moving cat.

Man. Yes, unfortunately we used to hunt and eat horses and as a result there is an in built wariness of our upright outline and two legged movement!

The instinctive response for any prey animal faced with a potential predator is to run away or escape, if they didn't they would be caught, eaten and would not pass on their genes to the next generation (hence only the smart, reactive and aware individuals tended to stay alive long enough to breed).

As the horse evolved their ability to respond with lightning reactions to potential threats improved and this pattern of behaviour can be seen in other prey animals that have a large number of predators that feed off them, such as rabbits. If you start to imagine your horse as a giant rabbit rather than your baby boy or girl, you just might begin to see the world as they do, a minefield of threats and dangers to be negotiated with great care.

Horse can learn to ignore their instincts but this has to be done through careful training and a trusting relationship. It can be done though otherwise they would never let us on their backs in the first place. Most people understand this and how difficult it is for a prey animal to work closely with a predator such as ourselves but we often forget and become complacent that our "bombproof" horse will sometimes receive a trigger that sets into motion the millennia of pre-programming. Take the major culprit the white plastic bag. Many horses are predated by ambush predators and often the only warning they would get is a quick glimpse of a flash of the white tooth of the predator as they snarled to pounce, or even just a flash of the white of their eye. All horses will react to the colour white and it is even used by other prey animals to warn of predators, the white rear end of deer and of course the white tail of the rabbit. Any white object moving or stationery can trigger the flight or evasion response of the horse, especially if they are taken by surprise.

It doesn't stop there though, even common, everyday objects that the horse may see and never react to, if moved, can trigger extreme reactions. Why should this be the case? Remember the need of the horse to explore their surroundings? This is not just a meaningless exercise for the horse, it is absolutely vital that a horse builds up a detailed mental map of their territories. This would include places to eat, drink, escape routes, places of danger etc and nature has provided the horse with an almost photographic memory. They have the ability to notice in finite detail the world around them and they are only comfortable knowing everything is in its place. If one thing moves or changes then it must be treated with suspicion. This harks back to the "picture" in their mind of their safe territory, a strange object suddenly appearing may well be a predator, especially if it matches any of the pre-programmed predator shapes. It also relates to familiar objects. A horse may be comfortable with the traffic cones in the school, but if they meet them suddenly on the road then it is a different story, especially if the cones have not been there before.

If we take all of this into consideration it is remarkable that many horses are able to cope with the demands we put upon them and the ever changing environment they live in. It is testimony to the resilience and adaptability of the horse and their intelligence that they can overcome this programming and work with us. What would help them though is if we understood that we are in fact working with a giant timid rabbit!

So how do we start to venture into the world of the horse and try to establish a relationship? First we must have a set of rules, similar to those a horse will have in their wild herd. What I find truly amazing is that horses the world over have the same set of rules of behaviour between themselves irrespective of their country of origin, whether they are wild or domestic, live large groups or small families. As a foal grows up he must learn the rules and the most important rule is good manners. No horse will tolerate what they deem as rude behaviour from another and often older herd members will help discipline unruly behaviour. This can be seen in those domestic herds that are as close to a wild herd as possible. If things get out of hand an older or higher ranking horse may well step in and sort it out, it is vital that the harmony of the herd be maintained. Perhaps we should take a leaf from their book, often the most ill-mannered of horses with people is the epitome of politeness and etiquette in the company of other horses and this speaks volumes with regards to human/horse relationships.

Here an older mare splits up a yearling (left) and two year old (right) who were about to descend into a kicking competition.

How many times have you watched someone being dragged about by their horse and thought to yourself how ill-mannered their charge was being and how your precious little darling would never behave in such a way. How often have you heard people say, "I want to buy a youngster who has not been *wasted* by stupid people" and agreed with them without realising that all the *wasted* horses of this world were once innocent youngsters who may well have been bought by someone with the very same notions.

The biggest problem seems to stem from the fact that to a horse everything is very black and white, there are no grey areas. You are either allowed to do something in a herd or

you are not. However, we complex humans can sometimes have ever changing goalposts which seem to vary from situation to situation or person to person. We have the ability to "lie" be it "white lies" or not we can bend the truth to suit our own ends or cause trouble where horses on the other hand never lie.

What we need to do is base our rules of behaviour or manners on what horses have agreed between themselves. The first rule is one of personal space. A horse will not invade the space of another without invitation or intent to dominate. If a horse is invited into personal space it may be to groom a friend or play with a friend, for whatever reason there are subtle exchanges of posture which amount to a conversation along the lines of, "Hi there, do you want to play with me?" The answer will either be yes or no. If the answer is no and from a subordinate the next comment might then be one of mild annoyance or aggression from the horse that wants to play in order to show his or her displeasure at being turned down. This will either cause the other horse to move away or give up and turn to play for a short while. If the answer is yes then serious horseplay will begin. When horses play (especially males) it can get pretty rough as it is basically stylised fighting, it will almost always finish with one of the horses backing down and submitting and ending the play session, so there is almost always a "winner". If it is the subordinate who is asking for play and the superior says no then the subordinate will either walk away or stay quietly grazing or standing next to the superior just being a friend.

Horses don't have to approach each other for a purpose they may simply want to hang out and be with their friend, but either way they will always ask politely to approach another. If a horse is not polite and barges through another's space with a "get out of my way or I will hurt you"  attitude they will either be met with a very aggressive response and be "put back into their place" or the others will move away showing deference and submission. They may well get a nip or bite by the dominant bully to underline his or her authority. What you will find is that most horses avoid the company of such a bully as it is just too much hassle and they are too unpredictable.

Let's look at this scenario now when the other horse is substituted for a human. Most people are completely unaware of how horses encroach on their space and push them around, in short most horses are used to treating people in much the same way as the equine bully treats the herd. They may ask to approach your space but most of us are not clued into the subtle signs and miss them altogether. Some horses take this as an invitation and move in anyway, this can also lead them to think you are being submissive to them. Depending on what they want will depend on what happens next. The horse may ask to play, this may begin as gentle nuzzling or nibbling of clothing or hands, or "punching" with their nose or head into your face. You may push them away (this is part of the push me push you game) and they come right back at you with an increase of intensity. This shove game could go on for some time till the horse gives you a nip or bite and you lose your temper and either hit them or chase them away, you may even become frightened and move away from them. A horse will be confused by a playmate that has suddenly become violent and angry, especially after inviting play and may regard the human as an unpredictable bully. If the human moves away, then the horse is the winner and they have established a higher ranking over the human.

Then you can get the other extreme where a human will come in with all guns blazing and push and shove the horse around, moving into their space without asking or being polite then punishing the horse if they don't move quickly enough. This the action of a bully and although the horse's may comply, they will avoid the company of a human bully as much as an equine bully showing very little trust or confidence in them.

If you watch a herd long enough you will see that there are some individuals who hardly ever "play" with others.

 They may still be well liked and will socialise with friends and may even be relatively high ranking, they simply don't want to play and they make this clear in a subtle but definite way if a horse approaches them. Other horses respect this and will always be polite around these individuals often choosing to follow them and want to be with them. This seems to be because they are very consistent in their behaviour and steady and clear in their communication. These are the individuals that we should model ourselves on. We are not physically able to deal with horses on an equal basis and so must make it clear what is acceptable behaviour. Humans should not indulge in horseplay as seen between to male horses as we would be seriously injured or killed. As long as we make this clear to the horse then that is perfectly acceptable to them. The key to developing this relationship is to be consistent. Decide how you would like your horse to behave and be consistent with the rules, never change them, never say "oh it's all right to barge into me today but not tomorrow." It doesn't matter what your set of manners are between you and your horse as long as you both stick by them. Remember that no one likes a horse that bites, kicks, barges, bolts or is dangerous in any way, these are the *wasted* horses that will eventually be thrown away. These are the horses that will be sent away to be "sorted" and often the only "sorting" required is for the trainer to establish the ground rules and be consistent. These ground rules can be applied for example when the horse tries to barge. The trainer will already have taught the horse to

move out of their space (there are so many different ways of doing this that it is not possible to list them all) so if the horse tries to move into the trainer or past them they will instantly be asked to move back. It doesn't matter what rules you use as long as they are suitable and non-abusive and that you are consistent in your application of them.

So it is clear that one of the best ways of deciding what good manners are is by observing equine etiquette in a herd. We can model our own set of rules around these and ensure that our rules are in line with everyone else who is working with our horse. We must also be careful never to assume that other people have the same set of rules, for example, some people feed tit-bits some people don't. Never give a strange horse a tit-bit without first checking with the owners if this is acceptable or not as this may be a direct infringement of their set of rules of good manners. What is important is that you keep in mind that "God forbid" you may have to sell or move your horse on should your circumstances change and it is therefore vital for the well being of your horse that they have universally acceptable good manners. For example they don't bite, kick or barge in any way, this will give them a better chance of a good home and fair treatment.

It is very difficult for some humans to instil good manners in their horses as they are sadly lacking in good manners with other humans. It is therefore important that you look closely at yourself and be honest with what you see. It may be necessary to change how you approach others, how you behave in society and how you interact with your own species before you can help your horse. If you are not sure about your own nature then I suggest you look at your horse, I was told by an old horseman, "If you want to know about a person, then look no further than their horse" and never a truer word was spoken. It is very difficult for people to admit their shortcomings but in order to grow and develop we must understand our weaknesses and work towards developing our strengths and creating balance.

Horses are honest and open and you should follow their lead in this respect. Try not to tell lies, try not to think badly of others. Be yourself, if you don't like someone or something then simply avoid association and never say or do anything to cause trouble or create ill feeling. This is easier said than done and there are many people who simply don't want to change their ways. This is perfectly acceptable, but don't expect the horse to show good manners if you will not.

We have a very powerful ethos in the Equido system:-

- Watch your thoughts
- They become your words
- Watch your words
- They become your actions
- Watch your actions
- They will dictate your future

Chapter Three
From the Ground Up

We all know that anything with an unstable foundation will not stay upright for long and this is one of the most important areas for horsemanship. From an equine point of view, their legs and feet are vital to their survival, without a good strong sound foot and leg the horse will not be able to travel to find food or evade predators and taking care of their feet is one of the most important things a horse can do.

Horses are not born with total "body awareness" and anyone who has ever watched a foal take its first stumbling steps will tell you the look of amazement on their faces when they see the large gangly back legs following them about! It does take time for a horse to learn that the legs are in fact attached to their own bodies and much of this is helped by the mare who will touch and nuzzle the foal all over. This touch sensation helps the horse to feel where their bodies begin and end and to connect with their own physical structure. It has been found that some humans are born with a difficulty in making this connection and it is known as "clumsy child syndrome". Often people with this syndrome take a long time to learn exactly where their bodies are and activities such as sport or dance help to develop this body awareness. Horses have the same issues. We all know the "clumsy" horse who is always getting himself into trouble, getting injured or falling over. It may be that these horses are in fact struggling to "connect" with their own bodies and for one reason or another may not be able to "feel" clearly where they are. In the wild, a horse such as this may have a very short life expectancy but in domestication there is a lot we can do to help develop horses such as this.

One of the ways we can do this is to use exercises to help the horse understand where their feet are. "My horse is already trained, why do I need to bother with boring stuff like groundwork? That's for babies and novices isn't it?" How many of us have heard this statement or something like it or even worse have even thought it? Quite a few no doubt, myself included and yes it is true that if your horse is already schooled or competing you might not think it necessary to go over simple basics with him, but believe me, we all can do with a reminder of basics now and again.

Ever wondered why your jumping horse kicks out poles with little concern, or stumbles on uneven ground. What about your horse that is always getting their legs kicked or stuck in things? Could there be something you can do to help minimise the injuries and improve your jumping score?

It means a lot for a horse to be in control of their feet and often horses will control the movement (feet) of others to show their higher position in the equine ranks. By making a horse move their feet (either by asking them to walk away or move over) position in the herd can be established without the need for physical violence.

It is therefore a very important thing for a human to be able to control a horse's feet. This means that they can make their horse stand still or move a particular leg in a given way on command. It means a lot for the horse and has much more significance to them than just movement. The ability for a human to control a horse's feet will automatically put them higher ranking and hopefully will encourage the horse to give them respect and trust. What is very important is how the human controls the feet, obviously anything done by force or violence will have a very different meaning to the horse, similar to the herd bully for instance.

Considering how protective a horse is over their legs, think how difficult it must be to "give" their legs to us when we are picking out their feet or shoeing them. By doing this they are effectively giving up their ability to run or defend themselves and if you think for a moment that not so very long ago we were their predators it is a really big ask for a horse. Anyone who has worked with unhandled or youngsters will understand how difficult it can be for some horses to trust humans enough to allow them to handle their legs. This can be a very frustrating business for the human but a little understanding on our part as to how difficult it is mentally (as well as physically standing on three legs when you are designed to stand on four) for the horse to comply then perhaps we be a little more patient and forgiving of their mistakes, after all, we expect them to forgive all of our transgressions.

Another difficult issue many horses have is walking over different surfaces. Now, remember one of the most basic instincts in the horse is to keep their legs safe so if they are unsure of any new or strange surface they need to be given time to reassure themselves that it is ok. Often they would like to paw at the new ground, testing its stability and grip and more often than not we punish them for doing so and try to chase or force them to move on. A horse is never really satisfied with something unless they have touched it with their nose and the foot test almost invariably comes first. Most youngsters get a chance to grow up experiencing different surfaces such as grass, soil, tarmac, concrete, gravel etc. but some never get the chance to experience such things, some don't even learn that the ground is not always level.

After a very long time re-training and with patience, we finally reduced the six legs to four! Now he enjoys his new hobby of endurance riding.

We had an ex-trotter who had raced for five years brought to us for backing. His whole life had been, stable, flat turnout paddock of ¼ acre, horse walker, racetrack. Any road work he had done had been in a very flat area and so he had absolutely no experience of hills or slopes. Even gravel or stone tracks were a totally new experience for him. He had obviously never really learned where all his feet were and was quite frankly the most uncoordinated, clumsy horse we had ever met. We called him Six Legs because he would quite literally trip over his own feet whilst walking and fell over on numerous occasions. He taught us an awful lot about re-educating a horse on balance and feel and we spent a very long time on groundwork exercises, making him think about where his feet were and how he needed to place them to keep safe. In essence, what he should have learned as a foal was now happening to him at 6yrs of age and it took him considerably longer than a foal to really learn where his body started and finished.

His lack of understanding of leg placement meant he got into an awful lot of trouble with other horses and he would frequently come in with kicks and cuts on his legs when he had picked a fight and had moved his body out of harms way but left his legs in prime position. He now has very lumpy, bumpy legs but hopefully he has now learned to keep them safe!

Often we as humans fall into bad habits or lazy ways of doing things, just for quickness and we simply can't see any fault in doing this and our horses are exactly the same. For us humans our lazy habits are seen mostly when we drive our cars, because, quite honestly, how many of us drive the way we have been taught or the way we had to when we sat our tests? I know I certainly don't, and often it is the one time that we don't check our mirrors or are driving with only one hand on the steering wheel that we can get into bother. I drove my first car into a ditch because I took my eyes off the road to change a tape in the cassette player (yes I really am that old!).

The same can be said of our groundwork or manners in our horses. Often, as long as our horse does his or her job well and is no bother to work with, we let them get away with very small habits which if left alone can become not only annoying but dangerous as well. How many of us have a horse that won't stand still when being groomed and wanders aimlessly around the stable as we try to brush them. Now, they may not be running away from us nor may they be making our job particularly hard and we simply may not notice that we are forced to wander around after them. The same can be said when putting a rug on, how many of our horses walk away or around us as we put on their rug. Just because we are in a hurry and can manage to cope with this annoying habit doesn't mean it is ok. How much more time would be saved if we took the time to say "no, stand still, there is nothing to be afraid of." Believe me it is much easier to rug a horse standing still than one doing the wall of death in a box.

When we allow our horse to take this action we are saying to them that it is ok to decide where to go and when to go, even what speed to go at and this is fine, as long as you are ok about your horse making this decision. But problems may arise when you need to dictate speed, direction etc from the ground and you will find that your horse will not be listening to you or paying attention because quite frankly you have already allowed them to act this way. This becomes more evident when you are leading your horse. For convenience sake you maybe don't have time or can't be bothered to lay down strict ground rules for leading, you allow your horse to trail behind in a dream or charge ahead pulling you forwards as long as they remain with you and don't try to run away. But simple rules that require your horse to pay attention to you when being led can be a life saver as believe it or not, not all horses are clever and careful with their feet and can quickly get themselves into difficulty causing them to panic.

We are very strict on our ground rules with all our horses and each horse is led in exactly the same way with the same expectations required of them. The horse must walk calmly and quietly on the rope with a light feel and with their heads level with our shoulders. They must not crowd us, walk behind us, charge ahead of us or pull away. Each horse must match the pace set by the handler and sometimes we will underline this if a horse becomes pushy and rushed. In this case we stop and ask the horse to either wait or if really pushy they will be asked to walk back a couple of steps. The horse soon realises that the more they try to harass the handler to moving faster then the longer it will take to reach their destination and if they simply watch the handler and match their pace then all will be well. The same can be said of those horses who like to trawl along at a crawl, not paying attention, not focussed and quite frankly not caring where their handler is or what they are doing. These horses are immediately asked to liven up their pace with changes of direction and more energy put through the line to encourage their interest and get their focus. They must walk smartly and watch the handler, stopping when they do and changing pace if required. This will encourage the horse to take an interest and become more alert.

So why is this necessary? A perfect example of this was highlighted to us quite recently during the cold snap. Although grit had been spread on the main pathways leading to the field there was still a risk of slipping on the rock hard ground as the odd icy patch missed by the grit still remained. It was absolutely vital that all of the horses walked slowly and calmly, with their eyes and attention on the handler as they picked the best and safest route to the field. If any horse had misbehaved or not been paying attention then there was a real risk of slipping on the icy patches which could have resulted in injury. Because of our attention to detail when working with all our horses and the level of attention and respect the horses give us when being handled not one of our gang got into bother. Every horse walked slowly and quietly, sometimes having to pause whilst a route was picked out. Each horse was very aware that the ground was not entirely safe and that they must trust the handler completely and follow their lead. When you consider we have a range of horses from 14hh to 17.2hh with a variety of issues and problems, it was remarkable that all managed to match the slow creep of the handlers and not one was anxious or upset by the experience, in fact, it highlighted to them why we insist on our strict rules and so at last everything made perfect sense.

You just never know when you might need to insist your horse listen to you as intently when on the ground and so you really must practise the rules every day. Remember, horses like consistency, by being consistent in your ground work you just might be able to avoid a nasty accident in the future.

"My horse is too old to learn this new stuff, he is set in his ways" this can be a common excuse laid down by people but the truth is that it is not the horse that is set in his way, it is the owner.

We have a 27yr old who has had leading issues due to his being partially blind in one eye. He arrived with a tendency to rush and barge. He often swung his head round and could knock into you or rush past you in a panic. If he caught a glimpse of something unexpected he could suddenly slam on the anchors and go into reverse.

All of these issues were addressed in the first few weeks of his stay here. If he rushed he was taken back to the start or backed up. If he tried to crowd you he was pushed back to a respectable distance. If he ran backwards he was always on a long enough rope to allow him space to back away from the scary object but still be attached to the handler.

The important lesson he learned from us was that we did not get upset when he got it wrong, we did not get angry and shout at him, we understood his problems and we were willing to listen and try to help him. Because our energy was calm and understanding and he did not frighten or worry us he too began to relax as he understood we could be trusted to keep him safe and slowly he began to trust us. By the time the icy weather came he had almost forgotten his habits of the past and it was a real pleasure when I led him out the stable and simply said "slowly now" he immediately realised he had to move very slow and follow me and this he did without fear, worry or arguments. He doesn't always get it right, but he does most of the time and truly shows you can teach an old horse new tricks.

Equido teach how to achieve a light feel on the rope when leading your horse and a softness that comes from the inside of the horse as they relax completely and focus totally on what  you would like them to do. It is so important that we ourselves remain polite and reasonable in our requests as this will encourage the horse to respond with equally reasonable and polite movements. It is only when we become demanding and push for a result that the horse will tense and brace and become resentful. We have seen with many of our remedial horses that they need time to let go of previously held beliefs that humans don't listen and are unfair, it may take years for a horse to learn to trust again and be willing to let us in. It humbles me that so many horses that have had such difficult times can be so forgiving. We let them begin their journey right at the beginning with the basics of being led, the same way you would teach an innocent foal to be led and handled. By taking them back to the very basic work we give them a chance to show us where it all went wrong and where they got confused. You will be very surprised to learn that more often than not the horse has simply never been taught these ground rules ever when working with humans and they simply did not know any better.

It helps the horse to understand that there is a point to their work. Most horses cannot see any use in running round in circles on the end of a rope, to them it is a needless waste of energy. Sometimes simple exercises, such as yielding the quarters, make no sense to the horse until you are grooming them or moving past them as you muck out and you ask them to move just their quarters over whilst they are eating their hay.

Backing up can be another mystery to the horse as being made to go backwards is quite a submissive movement. However, if you practice asking your horse to back up a few steps whilst you open the gate/stable door etc then it all clicks into place as they realise the practicalities of it all and that you are not just being a bully. Of course, asking your horse to back up over an excessive distance has a different meaning for them altogether and depending on how you do this and what intent you have behind it will make a considerable impact on the horse and your relationship with them.

This foot control can be practised with even the youngest of foals, as soon as they are old enough to be led then they are old enough to learn. Remember, mum won't allow her foal to invade her space or move where she doesn't want them and she is very quick to get her offspring's attention and respect. When a mare says "follow me now" she means it and the foal knows exactly where they should be. By building up this trust with the human combined with a healthy respect for who is in charge it can mean so much if your youngster gets themselves into difficulties.

Our 17month old is a confident, cocky little filly with a knack of getting herself into trouble. She is very clever and is always on the lookout for some game to be getting up to. As she is the only foal the nearest horse to her in age is 3yrs old, she does get spoiled a bit by the others but they do their best to keep her in her place. Right from the word go (as soon as she was weaned) she was shown exactly the same groundwork rules as the adult horses and she was handled and her feet trimmed etc. As a result she sees her humans (or should that be slaves) as part of her family and she totally trusts us when she gets herself into a pickle. One day we noticed her wandering about the field wearing a rather strange contraption. She didn't have a care in the world and was in fact quite pleased with her new attire. We realised she had somehow got herself stuck inside one of the light weight plastic ringfeeders which was now completely stuck and looked like a giant hoola-hoop. She noticed us and stood quietly to pose for a picture and trusted us completely to get her out. She did not move a muscle as we unscrewed the partition, twisted the unit round, flipped it over her head and carefully lifted her feet out. All her handling had made it very clear to her that we were only there to help and that she must surrender herself to what we asked of her and she would be fine. Anyway, she felt it made her bum look big!

Of course you must understand that groundwork does not necessarily mean grinding away at set exercises or making undue demands on a horse all the time. We would all get very annoyed very quickly if we had to recite our alphabet every day twice a day for the rest of our lives and in fact would then try to deliberately get it wrong just for entertainment. The same can be said of the horse. Once they have grasped the concepts of groundwork then they may only need reminded say, once a year or when necessary. But groundwork also serves to train us in our behaviour as well as the horse and so we must pay close attention to our groundwork as much as the horse and to evaluate on a daily basis how consistent and safe are we being. As I have said before there is no right or wrong way but the way that works for you and your horse and you can have your own set of rules. However, it pays to evaluate how much control your rules give you and if they really will help or hinder your horse in an emergency.

Chapter Four
Learning to Listen

One of the most important lessons Equido will teach you is the art of listening to your horse, but what does this really mean? We are constantly reminded to "pay attention" when working around animals and we are told frequently that the horse is an unpredictable animal with highly tuned flight instincts. We know that any prey animal has highly tuned senses that are basically switched on all the time. This means that their hearing, sight, smell, touch and even taste are constantly on "alert mode" feeding an endless stream of information to the brain ready and poised to take action to avoid a predator. When one of these "perimeter alarms" is activated there is a pre-set response already hard wired into the horse that will kick in even before the brain has analysed the information. In other words, the nervous system of the horse will initiate a preliminary response to flight even before the brain has analysed the information and assess whether or not flight is really necessary. This can happen in a millisecond and will of course vary from individual to individual. We all know of the "silly" horses who are paranoid about everything and spend their entire lives strung out being hysterical over anything and everything. Then there are the "bombproof"

types who would literally need a pound of dynamite under their tail to promote any movement whatsoever. All of the information that the senses are sending to the brains of both these very different types of animals is the same, the difference is in how it is acted upon and this depends very much on the evolution of that particular type of horse.

The evolution of the horse is very well documented but as man began to domesticate the horse there were four main types of equines that were being used. Two of the modern equine types of Equine Caballus are the pony types classed as Pony Type 1 and Pony Type 2. Pony Type 1 is slightly built with a lighter frame, thinner skin and other adaptations to a hot dry climate. Pony Type 2 is heavier and more solidly built, with a thick dense coat, the ability to lay down fat reserves very quickly and other physical adaptations to deal with cold wet conditions.

These pony types are relatively unchanged from their primitive ancestors and are highly adaptable animals with a very hardy constitution. They are perfectly designed to live in the open elements and surviving on very poor and sparse conditions.

Pony Type 1 can live in the most arid and inhospitable desert environments seeming to be able to survive on dry twigs and coarse grass

They are able to live off these fat reserves in almost artic conditions when food is not available due to heavy snow.

Pony Type 2 can deal with extreme weather conditions and freezing temperature, being resistant to the elements with their specially adapted coats and fat layers.

These types have never adapted to the digestion or rich grazing or concentrates and feeding of such can result in their susceptibility to endotoxaemias such as laminitis, obesity and intolerance of certain drugs.

The third and fourth type of Equine Caballus is horse type one and two. These animals were developed from the pony types, and fine tuned for either slow steady draught work or fast hard ridden work.

What is almost identical in both Pony Type 1 and Horse Type 1, Pony Type 2 and Horse Type 2, is their responses to the alert signals given off by their senses to possible dangers. In hot dry conditions both the Pony and Horse Type 1 have no need to conserve energy to provide heat or fat reserves and will therefore have the original response to danger with their nervous system going into flight mode very quickly before the brain analyses the situation fully, in other words they run first think later. These would be called the hot bloods in the equine world. The Pony and Horse Type 2 on the other hand are masters of conserving energy for it may mean certain death to waste energy reserves in running away from a stimulus via the senses that may not be necessary. These types have an over ride mechanism built in where their brain (depending on the strength of the stimulus from the senses) will analyse the situation and decide if it is necessary to take action, in other words they think first and run later. These horses would be called the cold bloods of the equine world.

Now, most horses today are a mixture of these types and as such most, like the cold bloods, can actively over ride their pre-programmed response to a certain extent. Many do not and it is arguable that they choose not to do so rather than are unable to do so. Sometimes however a horse that is troubled psychologically is unable to over ride this automatic response to perceived threats and will revert back to being reactive, either through biting, kicking, bucking, bolting, rearing etc as their automatic defences are triggered and they are unable to control themselves. This can have a major impact on us in our day to day dealings with such animals.

The horse is very much a here and now animal. For many the past is irrelevant (this is not to say they don't remember, quite the contrary, horses have a very good memory, but they are not normally hung up in the past unless there has been a real trauma in their lives and this is why horses are so forgiving) and the future does not exist as far as they are concerned. Now, again this does not mean they have no concept of future outcomes for their actions (I am going to be really controversial now, so not like me!) we all know of the little clever clogs who know full well that if they open the stable door and go into the feed room they can steal some food. This means they fully understand the chain of events they need to go through to get a future result. There are many examples we all have experienced that proves horses do have a concept of how their actions can influence their future, what I am trying to say is that horses are happy to experience and live in the present. Yes they may choose to act in the present in such a way as to affect the future, but they don't spend their time wishing for future things to happen, they simply go along with the flow and live in the moment. In order for them to do this safely they are fully alert to everything around them at all times.

Now, where do we dumb humans come in! We often spend our time worrying about things that have happened or dreaming about things that might happen and as a result we are often so preoccupied mentally that we miss what is going on around us. This can have a devastating result, especially if we are driving a car! One thing horses can and do try to teach us is to be aware of what is going on around us at all times. This must be applied fully when you are in the prescience of an animal that is in just such a state. In order to be as aware as horses we must allow our senses to be open to the environment around us at that moment in time. Focus on what is, not what has been or may be. This will allow us to glimpse into the world of our horses and it can teach us to be so super sensitive and alert that we will begin to really "hear" what our horses are saying without even realising it.

An example of this happened only recently to one of our staff. One of our remedial horses still occasionally lapses into a "zone" where he becomes distant as though remembering his troubled past. When in this zone he will sometimes kick out at an imagined threat. This horse has been improving on a daily basis and is almost "normal". However, one of our staff had went into the paddock to catch another horse and, passing close to the troubled horse who had been standing quietly dozing, he sensed a change in the energy from the troubled horse. Our staff member did not have time to analyse what exactly he had picked up, but because we practise being as aware as a horse he sensed a tightening of the troubled horses back, a slight tension in his stance and our staff member promptly stopped and stepped back quickly, his body reacting before his brain had even noticed. He had done this just in the nick of time as the troubled horse had gone into his "zone" and had lashed out at thin air, just within the range of where our staff member would have been had he continued walking.

It was a sobering reminder to all of us that it is often when we become complacent and unfocussed in our handling of the horse that we are most likely to be injured.

Often it is the safe, reliable stalwart of a horse that takes you unawares and injures you, not because they were being bad, but because we were being complacent and did not listen to the animal who is highly tuned, highly sensitive and totally switched on.

With the help of Equido training you will begin to find yourself walking in a world you didn't even know existed. You will begin to "see" things you had previously been oblivious to and sometimes you might get a bit of a wake up call. We have begun to see what it means to be a horse and what their values and goals in life are. We are also beginning to understand how they view the world around them and what their priorities are. Hopefully we are beginning to make progress in our understanding and working relationship with our horses and now they might well be opening up and trying to show you what their fears and issues might be.

In the past the horse was regarded as a beast of burden, there to suit the whims of man and be used as we see fit. They were not given any rights, they were not regarded as being able to think or even feel. They were used till they could not work any more then they were cast aside and destroyed. The horse did not have any say in who owned them, how they were kept, how they were treated or even how they would die. They had in effect no freedom and were no better than slaves to our industry. And yet, throughout this we still had a secret admiration for the horse, there were men and women amongst us who sought to make the horses lives less miserable and to try to educate people into caring for them better.

It is a disgrace that sometimes outdated ideas and methods of keeping horses are still practised today and this is one of the main things Equido hopes to change. The health of your horse will dictate their ability to work and compete. This not only applies to their physical well being but also their mental state. Horses are very sensitive animals and are easily affected by the environments in which they are kept and the methods by which they are handled and treated. We should all strive to care for our horse to the best of our ability and ensure they are mentally happy. How can we do this? I know that many of you feel that in order for a horse to be brought to peak fitness that compromises must be made in their care and work. It may not be possible (so you might think) to let them have a "natural" life. It is possible and Equido teaches you how to balance the need to get a horse to peak fitness for the job required yet still keep them happy and satisfy their equine mental needs. There are more and more top trainers who are beginning to see the benefits of trying to give a horse time to be a horse, even some racehorse trainers now allow their horses time out in paddocks for free grazing.

In fact, the more time a horse spends out the better for the horse's health and fitness. Just wandering around the field and socialising will provide exercise enough and can even eliminate the need to go through the first 4 – 6 weeks of a Traditional Fitness Programme! This is great for those of you who work and who might not have time to exercise a stabled horse 2 – 3 times a day. Sometimes we have to look beyond the "grass belly" (a perfectly natural thing for any horse) and see that they are in fact toned and muscled with very little effort from us. If you are really concerned about exactly how much your horse eats etc you can still allow them freedom in all weather paddocks with access to roughage on a controlled basis.

They can then be turned out with companions to "forage" for bulk (things like feed balls can stimulate this) and satisfy their equine need to wander and browse. Sometimes a few hours a day of liberty like this can mean so much for a horse in a tough competition job and can keep them relaxed and fresh for their work.

Now in this 21st century we should be able to apply our allegedly superior intellect to the task of reaching a compromise in what our horses want from life and what we want from the  horse. By reading this book you have already begun to "listen" to what the horse is trying to say to you. Yes it would be fabulous if all our horses could roam free, but this will never be realistic in our modern world. So what can we do?

Open airy stables looking out over a green tidy yard and arena can give your horse a real sense of space, even when they are stabled.

If you are lucky enough to own or rent your own yard or field then you are already well on your way to making things more "natural" for your horse. You might not have the luxury of being able to graze your horses all year round and you may have to "save" your pasture for the summer. In this situation you might be able to put down an "all weather" surface over an area where your horses could roam all day instead of standing in a box. If you replace the word Stable or Box for Prison in your vocabulary and then chat to your friends about how your horse spends 24hrs a day in his prison you might start to get an idea of what this means to a horse. Remember, they are animals evolved for open grassland, they are by nature claustrophobic, they would not willingly put themselves in a place where they cannot flee to escape predators and even though they may appear "content" tucked up in your 12ft x 12ft stable, the horse will be suppressing stress and anxiety about the whole situation. If you left the stable door open you would probably find that the horse would rather be outside in the open than in their stable. This might not apply to all individuals and there may well be horses out there who are happy to stand in a box, what I am suggesting is that this might not be the norm and that those individuals are the exception not the rule.

For those owners who do not have their own place and who are subject to the rules of the Livery yard they are on, things might not be so easy. It is very difficult to get a good yard that tries to work in the most natural way possible. More often than not the best yards hardly ever have any spaces because people just don't want to leave, this doesn't mean you should compromise what you want for your horse, instead you should shop around for something suitable. Isn't it worth that extra 15 – 20 mins drive if you  can put your horse on a yard which is designed to best meet the needs of the horse. In today's competitive market it pays for a yard to know what their clients want and if you make it clear by voting with your feet then perhaps things will begin to change.

If your horses are able to have liberty for at least half the day the impact on their mental well being will be enormous. This is especially apparent in competition horses who have a highly stressful job. Often a few hours a day at liberty (this does not mean in a horsewalker or treadmill) can prevent stress induced vices such as windsucking, cribbiting, box walking etc. Combining this with ad-lib hay or haylage might also minimise conditions such as gastric ulcers. It doesn't matter if you have to limit the amount of hay, making it harder for the horse to eat a small ration quickly is easy, place small haynets around the turnout area or spread their hay around the area so they have to "pick" at it. However, there is now evidence that horses who are fed small forage rations in small holed haynets or devices designed to make it difficult to get at the food, can in fact be put under even more stress.

So what does Equido teach us? We promote the ad-lib feeding of bulk and roughage such as hay or haylage. I know that there may be many of you now thinking, "I can't do that! My horses will just eat and eat till he/she explodes!" Let me tell you what we have found. By listening to our horses we know that they are designed to eat for at least 20hrs a day (my horse can manage 25hrs a day!!!). They are designed to eat grass and other tough to digest food, they are not designed to eat concentrate feeding that we give in a bucket. We have had horses brought to us with "weight" issues and we still feed them ad-lib roughage, as much as they can eat at all times. Initially these horses are astounded by the constant supply of something that was once denied them and they do make a pretty good attempt at emptying the racks. You should see the looks on their faces when we fill them up again just before they are completely empty. This eating feast usually lasts no more than 2 days by which point the horse is so sick to the back teeth of trying to munch his or her way through this never ending food source that they actually begin to ration themselves. We have found that horses who are "greedy" are usually made that way by being rationed, they are almost in a state of panic to eat as much as quickly as possible before it disappears. In the wild the horse has their food all around, yes they may have to work to find it, but generally they are free to eat whenever they want., what is unnatural and stressful for them is when bulk food is denied for periods of time. This combined with restraint in a stable or small paddock, causes the horse to become anxious and over zealous at feed times. We feed very little hard feed, much less than you would normally recommend.

We do this because we have had our bulk feeding analysed and it contains virtually everything our horses need nutritionally.

Out of curiosity we weighed how much roughage one of our "greedy" horses actually ate per day and it was just under 2.5% of their bodyweight, the correct amount (this

horse did not get any hard feed),. This "greedy" horse was never starved and was fed ad-lib. Over time, because the horse was worked but fed only roughage, he did begin to lose weight and regain his correct condition score. We had actually managed to achieve this not by starvation but by feeding natural food freely and allowing the horse to work things out for himself. Eventually we may need to feed more concentrate if the workload demands more energy, but to be honest, the horse is just as fast, fit and strong as other more "traditionally" fed horses.

This horse made us all really think and, out of curiosity, this winter we did not increase our concentrate feeding like we normally do to "keep them warm" but instead kept all of the horses on summer rations. (There were two exceptions to this, a 35yr old that has bad teeth and struggles to eat hay or haylage and a thoroughbred who also has bad teeth). What we have found is that not one of the horses suffered from this and they are all looking perfectly fit with good overall body condition, not too fat and certainly not thin. When we thought about it clearly, it all made sense. The horse is a superbly designed animal for living out doors and most breeds are excellent at maintaining weight and condition even in extreme weather. There are of course exceptions to this and a competition animal will need extra feeding to compensate for the energy used up and will of course need to be clipped and therefore rugged to compensate for their lack of hair and insulation. But the honest fact is that most horse owners simply do not work their horses hard enough to merit the amount of extra rich feeding they are giving their horses.

In the wild the horse will have a high fibre diet and during the summer months their bodies are designed to lay down as much fat as possible to prepare for the winter. I liken this to the human owner who stocks up on winter feeding to see them through the cold months. The horse's bodies will lay down the fat deposits on areas most likely to be exposed to the elements and it is on this fat supply that the horse will rely on during the freezing temperatures of winter. The fat also acts as an insulating barrier which protects the vital organs from the "chill" factor of the elements. Again you can liken this to the human owner who buys the very latest super cosy, snuggie, quilted, extra warm rugs with extra fleece lining for their horses just before winter.

Wild horses will drop a dramatic amount of weight during the winter, especially if it is long and hard. They grow a thick layer of hair which can be fluffed up to trap air which is then warmed by their bodies (similar to the very latest technology in rug design for super lightweight extra togg rugs!). The horse has natural designs in place which our modern science simply cannot compete with. There are of course exceptions to this rule, for example the breeds or types who are designed to cope with hot arid environments. In these cases it is of course important that we help their natural limitations with our man made equipment, especially in our cold, damp country that we keep them in, as I am quite sure they would migrate to warmer climates if given half a chance!

Then there is the problem of our perceptions of cold and the horse's. Now, there are a lot of humans out there who work outside for most of the day and it is very obvious to them that other people who work indoors a lot or in offices etc are simply not "hardy" and "feel" the cold more than they do. Even us feeble humans can become immune to lower temperatures to a point and we scoff at the "soft" people who are shivering whilst we walk about in a T-shirt. We also live in "heated" houses (usually heated to around 22°C) so when we walk out into the open air of say -1°C we are feeling an instant temperature drop of 21 degrees! Of course our bodies are going to be shocked, we will shiver and moan about how cold it is. The horse however does not live in centrally heated apartments (not all of them anyway!) and is already attuned to the ambient temperature. They simply do not feel the cold as dramatically as we do. (Even after this ridiculous cold snap of up to -16°C we found ourselves commenting on how *mild it was* when the temperature rose to 0°C!!!). Looking at our horses standing in the stables where they are sheltered from the elements and the temperature is at least 2 – 3 degrees higher than outside, we are imposing our impressions and feelings on them and we start to rug them up nice and warm!

Horses have a secret weapon up their furry sleeves. They carry around in them a built in central heating system! They are basically a fermenting gut on legs and the process of fermentation releases a lot of heat energy which warms the horse up from the inside out. Simply put, as long as the horse has enough roughage to stimulate the gut processes they will be nice and warm, especially if they fluff up their hair to contain this heat and minimise its loss. Then the human comes along and throws on a rug. This presses the hair flat and the horse cannot fluff up. This effectively removes an important insulating layer and unless the rug is "warmer" than the hair blanket the horse will in fact lose heat (all of us who put "lightweight" rugs on our horses are feeling a bit guilty right now as we may well be making our horse colder!).

The sad fact is that the affects of this "nanny" culture developing in the horse world means that horses that nature has designed to lay down their feedstore of "fat" in the summer, which should be burned off by the spring, are simply not burning off the excess fat. This means that they go into the Spring with a remaining store of fat. Their bodies however cannot undo the programming of millennia and will drive the horse to lay down more fat on top of the remaining. The result is that each year the horse is getting fatter and fatter and their health is suffering greatly. Illnesses such as laminitis is rare in the wild equine living on a sparse fibre diet as any excess fat is completely gone by Spring. We unfortunately often keep our already fat equines on pastures that are rich in nutrients and the poor horse is driven to eat as much as they can as their bodies cannot understand they don't need the fat reserves built up. Combine this with the

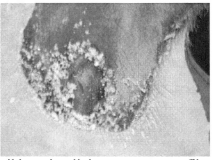

human taking away the need to burn fat to stay warm and provide nutrition and we have a frightening downward spiral.

What can we do then to help the horse? Firstly we can control their diet. If the horse is not working then they simply do not need to be fed any concentrates. It may be necessary to give them vitamin supplements and this may require to be mixed with something palatable but this can be provided by succulents rather than molasses sweetened feed stuffs that "look" pretty. (Remember a short walk of 1/2hr once a week does not constitute work!!). Feed good quality hay or haylage (even this can be controlled) and if you must give your horse something extra (psychologically for us not them) then make it a natural treat such as carrots or turnip etc.

Most horses will be stabled for at least part of the time (usually at night) over the winter as few places have enough grazing to cope with poaching. If the horse is stabled then fight the urge to throw on the duvet! Leave your horse au-natural and hairy. If your horse has to be worked then only give them a clip that is practical (do your really need a hunter clip to walk your horse an hour a week?). If you do have an overweight horse then you can give them a clip but not rug (I know this seems extreme but believe me it works). This simulates a really cold snap (like we have just had) and the horse's body will start to eat into its reserves to maintain body temperature. It is not easy to do this especially if you have a vast collection of every type of rug under the sun, but just imagine the money you will save when you don't need to buy the latest fashion of rug or this year's colours!!

By listening to our horses we have worked out how to give them the most "natural" lifestyle in this "unnatural" world. By learning to listen first we will begin to hear what our horses really need and then, we can begin to communicate with them.

Equido aims to teach you all about the psychology behind the horse, to understand exactly what makes them tick and how we can work with their nature and not against it. By listening to what the horse needs and wants and by trying to provide this we are on the first tentative steps on building a partnership with our equine friends. A partnership not borne from domination and force but from mutual respect and understanding.

Chapter Five
Learning Speak

Horses, because they live in large groups, must be able to communicate with their fellow herd members. Any social animal has some form of communication that can convey a whole series of messages to their companions. Horses have evolved an efficient visual communication system honed to a subtleness that is almost invisible to us, being large animals they are very spatially aware and communicate very effectively with visual signals through body posture, positioning of the ears, eyes, nose, tail and mouth. The whole array of signals is astounding and their varying combinations can allow the horse to express a full range of feelings and emotions to their companions with astonishing subtleness. The renowned author Michael Schafer has gone into great details and study of this language and his ground breaking book "The Language of the Horse" shows just how effective this postural and visual language is with its complex rules of etiquette and ritual.

Horse A on the left is more dominant than horse B on the right to underline this fact horse A has deliberately moved into horse B's personal space. A has inclined his head slightly towards B and is pushing with his body and eye contact against B (indicated by red arrow).

The picture of the two horses walking side by side demonstrates this quite clearly. Horse A has made his intentions quite clear to horse B. This has caused B to move away from him with a submissive lowering of the head, licking and chewing and neutral ears. This has avoided any unpleasantness and the social order has been confirmed. To many people watching they simply would have seen two horses walking around a field and completely missed the quick and rapid exchange of visual cues. This complex language is not totally inherent and many of the subtleties involved do have to be learned over a period of time (as can be seen by the lack of understanding of equine language demonstrated by some orphaned or hand reared foals). This does not mean that horses are holding conversations with each other and discussing the merits of the latest fashion in turnout rugs! This simply shows that horses can and do respond very effectively to visual cues and respond accordingly in order to maintain harmony in the herd and thus an easy life.

There is evidence that horses can communicate in ways which we ourselves cannot understand. During the late sixties and early seventies a gentleman called Henry Blake set out to prove, as scientifically as possible his belief that horses were capable of empathy or simple telepathy and

 could communicate with their fellows a range of concepts and abstract ideas. His earth shattering book "Talking with Horses" sent scientists into a frenzy as they replicated his experiments with very surprising outcomes. Henry Blake discovered that horses tended to form what he called "empathic bonds" this could be with one or more horses but they always seemed to be very close to one or at the most two others. We have all experienced this bond with our own horses who seem to team up and buddy around with specific individuals (sometimes not the sort of individual we approve of!).

What made Henry's experiments so exciting was that he found that horses in an empathic pair could "talk" to each other and express abstract concepts to their partners. One of his experiments was to separate one of the pair bond and remove the horse to a distance of about ½ - 1 mile away from his partner. There was absolutely no way that the horses could see or hear each other. At a specified time the stabled partner was "excited" usually by the expectation of feed and the resulting response of the removed partner was noted. Almost 90% of the time the horse removed from the experiment would become excited as though they too were expecting to be fed, this excitement continued until the stabled partner had been fed and his excitement subsided, at this point the removed partner returned to grazing. It became obvious to Henry that there was some form of communication other than the obvious visual cues going on and subsequent experiments carried out both by himself and other scientists have confirmed that in many cases there is a form of empathy (the communication of feelings) between very close partners.

Yes, it could be argued that perhaps the horses could "hear" the excitement caused by the other horse although not all of the horses being fed were vocal. Perhaps the removed horse was reading the body language of the observer or handler present, but the handler was not told when the stabled horse was being fed, they were simply asked to record the time and duration of any unusual behaviour shown by the horse.

The ability to learn and understand the language of your same species seems like a very logical thing to do, but we can also see that the horse, like other prey animals, has the ability to learn the languages of other species as well. For example, in the wild it was absolutely vital that energy is not wasted unnecessarily and there is no point in running from a predator that is not hunting. This can be shown by Zebras who are closely enough related to the horse to share an almost identical language. A zebra knows very well when a predator is hunting or not, they understand the language of the predator. They will keep a wary distance but will not run away wildly from the lion who is wandering across the plain looking for shade. They understand the language of a hunting predator and a relaxed "switched off" predator. They know the lion's basic language. Not only the lion's language, but the basics of all of the predators who prey on them. They even take this a little further and know the warning cries of other prey species, perhaps even what those cries mean, i.e. "lion", "cheetah", "snake", "hawk" etc. Prey species often graze together, and each species keeps a keen "ear" on what the others are saying. So, here you are thinking that only humans are smart enough to learn other languages!! Imagine, your horse probably knows more languages than you do!!

Now let's look at what the poor horse has to put up with from us. Remember, we were their predators so they already know when we are "hunting" and when we are "relaxed". I know you are all thinking that we don't hunt horses in our society, but let's look again at what physical signals a hunter might have. There would be tension in the body, muscles ready to pounce into action, a sharpness in the eyes, perhaps the lips would be tight, there would be a quickness to the movement, especially as they were about to strike and an underlying aggression caused by the adrenaline needed to fuel a pursuit and kill. Any predator showing some or all of these signals might well be preparing to hunt and any prey animal in the vicinity best be on alert or make themselves scarce.

Let's imagine you've had a bad day at work, or you are worrying and stressed about something. You've all heard the expression "coiled like a spring" and you all know that tense feeling you have when worried or stressed. Your face even becomes tight as you try to contain the frustration and anger in your mind. This in turn makes your movements sharp and quick and you can become irritable and angry over silly little things. Looks like you are showing a form of hunting mode. Now you want to "unwind" "relax" so you seek out the company of your horse (a prey animal) and cannot understand why they are misbehaving or wary of you!

The horse has no concept of what might be worrying you, they live in the moment and at that moment you are behaving like a predator. They may react in a variety of different ways, but they will be "switched on" to flight mode to some extent, ready to spring away from any perceived threat. That might just be the day your horse is "difficult" to catch, ever wondered why. Some horses can understand that although the human beside them is behaving like a hunter they themselves are not at risk, but no horse likes to be in an unpleasant atmosphere and some will switch off and simply "not want to know you" till your mood improves.

On the other hand, you might have had a brilliant day and things are good. You are relaxed and happy, you are content, in no rush to do anything in particular. When in the  company of your horse things just seem to go right, everyone is cooperating and you feel close to your horse who seems to really enjoy "hanging" with you and having fun. The horse sees a predator who is not hunting and who has now become his friend, he feels no tension from you and therefore no threat. This is when he is able to relax and try to work with you as a partner and not have any of the old fears of predation looming up. This is when the horse is happy to be in your company and even his eyes seem soft and open.

How many times have you heard people say "I like to go up to my horse to relax, this job is so stressful" now think how unfair it is that we turn up to our horse and expect them to deal with our emotions.

Having to deal with an owner's emotions is one thing but think what the poor horse has to put up with just being trained to work with us. We are a very verbal species with complex vocal languages that we predominately use to communicate with. We also have a very subtle and complex body language that we are unaware of but which we pick up on from each other subconsciously. For example, we all know the people who just don't like us for one reason or another. They might be polite and civil to us verbally but we get the hint that they don't like our company from the "vibrations" they give off. The horse on the other hand has a very complex body language and uses very few obvious vocal cues. Yet, think on how we train horses. We call them dumb animals, too stupid to even think properly but we expect them to learn a vocal language and understand what these sounds mean. "Walk On" "Trot On" "Stand" etc. We drill the horse constantly till they learn these sounds and more often than not, any hesitation or misunderstanding on the horse's part is met with swift punishment for being stupid or "trying it on". Now, think how some horses have been trained by humans using one language might get sold to another country where they are using a different vocal language. Initially the horse might not quite understand what is being asked of them but very quickly they learn what is expected in this new language.

The reason being is that the horse is not necessarily learning the vocal language but the intent, the energy, the meaning behind the noise. That is how horses can learn how to behave, this is far more subtle and clever than learning what a sound means, this requires a high degree of sensitivity to the meaning of a request or action. This would be fantastic if they were dealing with their own species, but the horse has to learn this level of subtlety when dealing with us, a different species altogether. So much for the dumb animal!!!

Not only is the horse required to learn what we mean, they are also required to go against the millions of years of evolution and learning that has allowed their species to survive and carry out actions that quite frankly to the horse seems like insanity. Remember how important it is for the horse to protect their legs? We expect them to go against all of their equine logic and go into a dark cramped box on wheels where they cannot run from danger. The ground (which for the horse must be stable and able to support their weight) will start to move and shake, almost throwing them off balance and making it difficult to stand. They are sometimes in almost complete darkness, there may be a small window of light but the landscape keeps moving and changing before they can properly see what things are. There are loud, sharp noises that cover any other sounds around them (now they cannot hear what is happening) and can even hurt their sensitive hearing. Strange smells of diesel or petrol fill their sensitive noses making it very difficult for them to pick up on any other scent. When it all stops they are released, not in their home territory that they are comfortable with and that they know, but somewhere different, sometimes with other strange horses who are also afraid and confused. So this animal, perfectly designed to be able to run for miles, hear the smallest whisper of sound, see clearly to their horizon for almost $360^{o,}$ memorise their territories to the tiniest detail and catch the faintest scent on the breeze, has been asked to give up all that nature had equipped him with and trust this predator/friend. How brave is this, how difficult is this, could you do it? Now have you ever wondered why some horses do not like to travel.

It is little surprise that some horses finally get to a point where they just can't cope. They may have been crying out for help for many years, trying to let the humans know that they don't understand and that they are afraid. Some people may pick up on this and may be able to help the horse before things get out of hand, but more often than not the horse is left to either cope with things the best they can or become labelled as "difficult" a "problem" or even "dangerous".

Not everyone working with horses wants to help remedial horses and this job can be very dangerous and is often a heart wrenching and thankless task. There is nothing more depressing than seeing a horse that has come back from the brink of a complete meltdown be given back to people who haven't learned and put the poor horse back through the trauma again.

You don't need to be working with troubled horses to want to learn the equine language. But by understanding even the basics of horse language you can understand your own horses better and hopefully hear when they are having problems and work through them together before they become issues.

Here one of our exchange students meets a horse for the first time at Happy Horse, the Equido centre for Spain. Dressed for the weather our Apprentice begins to work with the horse as a friend.

Equido is very, very thorough on teaching their students how to communicate with their horses through energy and body language. This helps the students be more aware of how their own state of mind can affect the horse in a variety of ways. A strong understanding of equine psychology helps the students create an environment and way of learning that is as stress free as possible for the horse and at least gives them a chance to work with us in the world we have created for them.

Walk with me. A meeting of minds.

Moving the feet. David asks the horse to follow his example and move her back leg back as he steps forwards. This builds a bond of respect and trust as David is always polite and gentle with his request, always giving the horse dignity.

Horses trained by Equido Instructors have the chance to start off on the right foot with humans and the owners of these horses probably receive more training than they ever imagined. The truth of the matter is, the horse is perfectly able to be a horse, but people need to be taught how to let the horse be a horse and still work for them. It is the people who probably undergo the biggest journey and it can be a very emotional experience for them, especially if their horse has always been labelled as a "problem" horse and who, they have discovered has really been a lost, frightened soul looking for a friend and help. It is our mission to help people and horses work together and to make the world a better place for both.

Horses are capable of learning such complex physical cues as used by riders and are usually so willing to please that they will struggle and sometimes even put their own lives at risk simply because the rider has asked them to. For example, horses are not natural jumpers (unlike deer etc) and to put their precious legs at risk by jumping large dangerous obstacles takes a great deal of courage and willingness to do as the rider asks. Think now of the times when your horse has swallowed their fear and carried out a request that you did not realise went against their sense of self preservation. Horses understand that we don't think like them and so they can be very patient with us and will make a great effort to get along with us and be obedient. It is in their very nature to want to be with a group and to have a friend and this allows them to try very hard, even if they are afraid, to do as we ask.

Equido will take your understanding of the horse to such a level that you will be able to work together so closely that you will only need to think a request (especially when

 riding) and your horse will respond. This ability to think with your horse is a real eye opener for a lot of students and can help bring them and their horses closer together.

Chapter Six
Working Together

The lot of a trainer is not always a happy one and we are constantly trying to help improve the communication between a horse and their owner. There are some instanced though when this can be nearly impossible. You know the old saying "You can lead a horse to water but you cannot make them drink" can sometimes be applied and can lead to disappointment for the trainer, especially when it comes to working with remedial horses. However, surprisingly enough it is rarely the horse that disappoints you. I was asked to go out and help catch a 4yr old mare that had not been caught in 2yrs. She was in a 2 acre field on her own and was happy enough to come over to a bucket but don't even think about touching her let alone putting a head collar on her or she would disappear in a cloud of dust.

Working in a two acre field is not ideal but as I had no other choice I worked the little horse carefully using advance and retreat methods. She began to respond so I gave the owner some exercises to do to allow the mare to tolerate being touched. I left the owner working on these exercises for a week. My next visit seemed to show that the owner had been doing exactly what I had asked her to do and the horse would now tolerate being gently touched on the neck whilst eating a feed. I worked with the horse using a bit of a sneaky technique of placing the noseband of the head collar over the top of the bucket so she basically put the head collar on as she ate. After a few attempts I managed to slip the head collar on and she was caught!

Surprisingly enough she was biddable and calm once the head collar was on and I realised that this was the object of her fear. So I advised the owner to leave the head collar on (not ideal in a field but essential in this case) and work with the horse every day. A week later I got a call again, disaster, the mare had apparently escaped into another field which was much larger and had got the head collar off. Back to square one I thought! When I went out the little horse came right up to me without hesitation and after around half an hour I managed to put the head collar back on (we had no food bribe) not a mean feat in a eight acre field with a bad to catch horse. The horse's behaviour and the owner's story were not really tying up. It was then that the owner said she wanted her backed to sell her. I advised the owner to bring the horse over to the livery yard I was working from and I would back her there.

She duly arrived (she had been led to the yard as she would not load or travel) and we began our work. Within a very short time the little horse accepted saddle and bridle and was able to long line. I found her easy to work with and eager to learn. She accepted her first rider without fear or incident and was working along happily in walk, trot and canter. Her fear of head collars remained though and you had to be very careful how you put one on, but she was improving. The owner watched everything we did and we taught her how to work with her horse. By the time our training was complete the little horse could be turned out in a herd in a fifteen acre field with no head collar on and be caught with no difficulty. She would walk, trot, canter and hack out alone or in company and at this point I gave her back to the owner. Much to my surprise the owner did not take her back to her original field or sell her, but kept her on the yard as another livery. This gave me the chance to see just how easy it is to undo all of the hard work put into a horse.

Despite the owner witnessing herself what had worked best for this horse she very quickly went back to her usually way of handling and working with her. Everything we told the owner she should not do with this horse she did and all the advice we gave her for working with the little horse was not carried out. For example, we stressed how important it was not to try to bribe her horse but to have a reward in the stable. The horse had learned very quickly to snatch a carrot from the hand then turn and run away. She however learned with us that in order to get her reward she had to be caught and lead into the stable. We taught the owner the correct body posture and movement required to keep her horse calm and not to frighten her and we stressed that on occasion she should just catch her horse, reward her then put her back out. We went into great detail how she should lead, handle and work with her horse and how important it was not to "discipline" her in a negative way. It was as though she had never heard us. She immediately went back to giving her horse a carrot when she was trying to catch her, she would ride her every time she was caught. She was harsh and abrasive with her in the stable and very impatient with her when handling her. As a result, within a very short time (a matter of weeks) the horse was becoming bad to catch again. It was a difficult lesson to learn as I had to walk past this little horse every day who would whinny at me almost pleading for the help and understanding that she thought she had found with us. As it was not my yard and the owner was not my client I could do nothing. I did however not hold my tongue when I walked in one day to find the owner beating her horse up in the stable with the head collar (I now understood the reason for the horse's fear). The crowning glory to the disaster came when my husband was out cycling past the field the horse's were in and saw a group of four or five people (the owner and her friends) herding all 10 horses (my own included) into a corner of the field with lunge whips and schooling sticks. The herd was frightened and the little horse was terrified. She had been turned out with catching straps (ropes/straps around her neck to grab hold of) and they still could not get near her. When my husband politely inquired if they would like him to bring the other horse's in to make things easier they were mortified, some were pathetically trying to hide the whips behind their backs, they had not recognised my husband because of the cycling gear he was wearing.

The owner moved the horse not long after the incident and I remember being at a show one day and spotted the little horse being ridden by someone at the other end of the field. The horse was excited and she accidentally unseated the rider. The owner tried to grab her as did some other people but she would not be caught. I shouted her name and she saw me on my horse and came running straight over and stood with me. I quietly dismounted and gave her a nice stroke for being good then led her back to the owner. I will never forget the look of betrayal on that little horse's face when I handed her back. I have since heard that the owner has been told by several instructors that the horse is not the problem, she is and she should sell the horse.

Why did the owner behave as she did? The only reason I could think of is that some people are so afraid of change or what they deem to be failure that they will continue to use their way (even if it is obviously not working) because they don't want the horse to beat them. These people just don't understand that the horse does not think this way and only wants to be understood.

Another incident comes to mind when a lady asked if she could bring her horse over for schooling as he was being naughty and she would like him "sorted out". When she arrived I sat down and took a lot of notes about their partnership. It became obvious that this lady seemed to take her pony to be "sorted" every few months or so to trainers and the previous two trainers she had been to I knew very well and highly respect.

Within a day or so of working with the partnership and after lengthy conversations with the owner it became very obvious that this was simply a mismatch of personalities. What had happened was that the owner's remit had changed. She had originally sought a horse for simple hacking once or twice a week, but now, as her riding improved, she wanted to do more, to school, maybe even do a little show. As her retirement approached she had visions of the two of them spending lots of time together and being the best of friends.

However, when she first looked for a horse she needed a tough little laid back character that was happy to fend for himself living out in all weathers in a field and only being attended to and asked to work three times a week at the most. This required a very independent character that was not reliant on humans or craved human company. The pony needed to be tough and laid back to the point of being lazy so that if the owner could not ride for a couple of weeks (which often happened) he would be neither up nor down about it the next time she got on him. He was quite simply, a happy hacker. The pony she had bought was perfect for the job and had been fantastic for the first few months of ownership. However, the lady had a difficult job full of responsibility and decision making and as such when she rode she simply did not want to have to think too much and was happy to let the pony make much of the decisions and "take care" of her.

I know from experience that if you go down this route then you better be willing to accept that the horse just might go on making the decisions even down to when it is time to go home and you simply cannot blame them for doing so.

It was when the lady realised she wanted more from the relationship and was pouring affection onto the pony (human affection, kisses, cuddles etc) that she noticed the change. Human affection does not make sense to a horse, they are horses not humans and not all of them tolerate such behaviour. This little horse was one of them, he tried to tell her as plainly as he could by nipping her, barging her out of the way, shoving her away with his head, or simply refusing to be caught. But she just didn't get it. Then she started to ask him to school! That was the final straw he must have thought! He began to be nappy, to buck, to make it clear to her that he did not want to be a school horse, it wasn't what he wanted to do.

When I explained this to the lady she was very upset. She had this romantic picture in her head of a "black beauty" scenario and I explained that there were plenty of horse's out there willing to fill that role but not this little guy, he was more of a "Jimmy Cagney" character more likely to punch your nose than give you a cuddle! She couldn't understand why she had been advised to buy such a pony, but as I pointed out he was exactly what she was looking for at the time, it wasn't his fault that she had changed the goal posts. He was a great little trekking pony and would be ideal in that situation where he didn't care who rode him as long as was hacking out with his equine buddies. He didn't crave human company and was a real equine survivor, why should it be his responsibility to change?

The lady went home and pondered her predicament. I heard through the grapevine that she took her "problem" horse to another trainer who surprisingly enough has advised her exactly the same thing. So she has spent a lot of money to get the same answer. I hope for her pony's sake that she will now take the advice and sell him to a home that is more suited to him. He is an extremely safe pony who would work all day on a hack if asked to, is surefooted and keen and who will ensure his rider gets home safely. What more can you ask of a pony? (Just don't try to kiss him!)

It is hard being a trainer and either watching your work undone or having to advise someone that they should part with their horse, but there are many more cases where everything just goes perfectly.

I had been asked to help this lady with her horse who had just bucked her off and fractured her ribs. She had taken the horse to several "top" instructors who had simply advised her that she needed the buck beaten out of her. I was the horse's last hope for if I could not fix her she would be put down (no pressure then!).

I was expecting to see a bad tempered, belligerent, single minded, obnoxious horse who simply did not want to work but what I found was the sweetest, gentlest, most willing and biddable mare I had encountered for a long time. Again, two and two were not making four! I carefully examined her on the ground and handled her and she was polite and willing to carry out my every request. As I watched her walk away from me I was shocked at how uneven her quarters were, I asked the owner to stand behind her and see how crooked her pelvis was. As I ran my hand over her back she almost sat down when I reached her loins. At this point I advised the owner she needed to consult a specialist veterinary surgeon as I felt there may be a problem in her hindquarters that was causing her to buck. She advised me that several vets had examined the horse and nothing had been found. I showed the owner again the horse's reaction when I put pressure on her loins just in front of the pelvis and this time the mare politely (but pointedly) lifted her hind leg and waved it at me in a warning. The owner was mortified as the mare never kicked out at anyone, I explained that the horse was justified in what she had done as I was obviously hurting her quite badly.

The owner took my advice and in the meantime gave me a video to watch of a lesson she had received from a top instructor not so long ago. I was horrified by what I saw. The instructor had got on the horse "to sort her out" as she was bucking every time she went into canter. He was beating the horse continuously with a schooling stick (used like a jumping stick) and she was obviously very lame in the back legs, a point that he was missing completely. The owner was crying and begging him to please stop hitting her horse and it was so appalling that I wanted to send the tape to the proper authorities.

I received a call from the owner a week later thanking me so much for my advice. A different vet had examined the horse and found she had very bad bone spavins in both hocks. The pain, he said must have been unbearable, especially when asked to canter with the pain shooting up her back into her pelvis. She had been trying to compensate by holding her pelvis crooked and as a result had caused herself even more pain. He was not surprised she bucked in canter and was amazed she would even carry a rider in walk or trot, what an honest little horse.

Six months later I received a call from the lady to say her horse had completed her treatment and had been given the all clear. She understood that the horse would still be afraid of the remembered pain and asked if I would take her in to re-start her in her training and help her overcome her fear. This we did and she trusted us completely and tried her hardest. She was perfect in her behaviour and never offered to buck once. The owner came with her for lessons and rode her according to our instructions and carried out our every request to the letter. About a year later I received a call from the same lady to say how grateful she was for saving her horse's life and to say that she was now a very successful dressage horse and they were both having a wonderful life together.

Thankfully there are more positive stories than negative simply because there are many more positive owners who actively listen to advice and are willing to make the changes needed to ensure their horse's success. It is up to the owner to work with the horse and to listen to their needs. As the old saying goes "You can lead a horse to water but you cannot make him drink", so would you be willing to take a drink if it was offered?

When horses come to us for training we often simply need to give them time to tell us their own stories. You can learn an awful lot from a horse if you listen carefully and we have had some really horrific cases of abuse (mental and physical) pass through our yard. Take for example Diablo.

DIABLO:- Diablo was a one day eventer (intermediate level) and was a very troubled and unhappy boy. He was a "product" that had a job to do and had been "produced" to a point of being mechanical. Since the age of 4yrs he had had little or no socialising with other horses, had been stabled 24hrs a day with turnout of around half an hour once or twice a week on his own. He was competed at a consistent level and did the best he could to perform well. He was ridden hard with spurs and liberal application of the whip as he started to become more and more shut down.

His behaviour in the stable left a lot to be desired. He hated himself, he hated his job, he hated people and he hated other horses. He would lunge and bite anyone or anything that passed his stable, he would turn round and kick at anyone entering his box. He was dangerous to be around and lethal to tack up having to be short racked to be safely handled.

His current owner could see the pain and suffering going on in his mind and out of sympathy and concern for his well being she bought him (for a very high price) to try to help him become a normal boy again. Full marks to his owner for her perseverance. The first step she took was to buddy Diablo up with her other horse and try to encourage him to learn how to be a horse again. She turned him out in a field through the day (it would have been too much of a culture shock to turn him out day and night) and slowly he started to calm down. He was still very aggressive to tack up but she persisted and took him on hacks, avoiding the school as much as possible and asking very little of him. He remained unpredictable in his stable, prone to biting and kicking and was still very shut down and withdrawn.

His owner had the chance of stabling at our yard and so our work with Diablo began. He arrived at the end of the summer with a bad wire injury on his leg. This required treatment and dressings to be applied daily and he had to spend time on box rest. Because Diablo had had a small taste of being turned out he reacted very badly to being cooped up in a stable. He had also found a new (and as he thought only) friend in his new owner's other horse and displayed extreme separation anxiety. So although he had improved, he still had a long way to go. We reached a compromise on the box rest by turning the round pen into a 12ft x 12ft steel cage. Diablo felt like he was outside as he could see all around him, feel the air and experience the elements yet his movements were restricted. This seemed to work and his leg healed up very quickly.

Diablo was psychologically damaged and did not demonstrate normal horse behaviour. He did not have any rhyme nor reason to his aggression but simply acted automatically. We first worked with him in hand in the stable, letting him understand how to move over when asked (without kicking out or trying to bite). It became very obvious that his aggression was defensive and as he began to feel less threatened he began to calm down. Being turned out in a herd was a big help but very frightening for him and he stuck close to his stable mate as slowly but surely he re-learned his own language.

One incident sticks out and highlights how little communication skills he had; when asked to move over in his stable one night he became confused and anxious. He wanted to do the right thing but simply couldn't work out what was required, he also wanted the handler to understand that he was not being bad and needed help, he began to demonstrate what is called "foal snapping" which is a mouthing behaviour as the horse appears to open and close their mouth with a licking motion. This means "please don't hurt me I am only little and don't understand" a very clear message from any foal to an older horse but this was being demonstrated by a 12yr old to a human in a desperate attempt to let the human know he was confused in the only language he could remember. I have never seen any horse, other than a foal or youngster, foal snap and this behaviour can easily be misinterpreted as an attempt to bite. Fortunately for Diablo his handler understood exactly what he meant and he quietly stepped to one side and let him work out the problem for a moment himself. Diablo realised what was being asked and moved over with a sigh of relief that at last a human had understood. This was one of his first attempts to communicate with and ask for help from a human.

Through time Diablo began to relax and mix with the herd. The other horses understood that Diablo was a little unbalanced mentally and was prone to "going off on one" with little provocation. They interacted with him when he was balanced and when he started to behave irrationally they backed off and left him alone. In this way Diablo slowly built up an understanding of what was acceptable behaviour and what was not.

His understanding in the herd corresponded with his understanding in the stable and he was no longer aggressive or defensive and started to seek out human interaction in a quiet and friendly manner. He was still defensive about having his rugs put on and had to be reminded verbally to "pay attention", he would then focus really hard and concentrate on not biting or kicking. It was obvious that he had to make a conscious effort not to reflex bite at the handler as the front buckles were done up. Over time he became used to not biting and has slowly forgotten the habit. He no longer kicks out at people in aggression but can still fly kick if he becomes stressed but this is not aimed at anyone or anything.

The biggest change in Diablo is his overall attitude to life. If you met him now you would see a happy face with pricked ears taking a keen interest in all that goes on around him and a large friendly eye. He actively seeks the company of people and is polite and affectionate. He can still be defensive with other horses too near him but he has found his own place in the herd and his confidence grows from day to day. He no longer shows any separation anxiety if his stable mate goes out for a hack and is far more relaxed and starting to enjoy life.

Diablo is an on-going case. He has been with us for two years now and is happy with himself, happy with people and almost happy with other horses. We are still working on him being happy about work under saddle but we are getting there. He loves to hack out and relax and so this gives us a good place to start from. Diablo will never be a "normal" horse as the psychological damage goes very deep. However, with the right handling and a lot of patience he will be a very happy horse who is no longer angry with the world.

For many horses and their owners life is a journey of experience and growth. Hopefully the things that horse and human learn help to make them better individuals and to be able to work together peacefully and in harmony. This may not have been the case initially and some partnerships require help along the way to bring them to their full potential.

GIGALO: Gigalo's story is somewhat different. When I first saw this horse and his owner in action it was during a two day clinic run by a trainer from England. His rider spent almost all of the two days in either canter or gallop in the arena as Gigalo found it almost impossible to offer anything but top gear. The instructor did not offer much help to the pair and as a result they did not progress any further and the partnership was near to breaking point.

Out of the blue Gigalo's owner contacted me and asked if I had any livery spaces available, I had one stable recently vacated and so the combination came to our yard for assistance.

The partnership between Gigalo and his owner was on really shaky ground, his owner loved him very much but also realised that if things didn't get sorted out soon there could be a serious accident as Gigalo was on the verge of being a bolter. At first glance Gigalo appeared to be a confident strapping personality and it would be easy to misjudge his temperament as being a "typical lazy cob". The truth could not be further from this. Gigalo was a very insecure horse, nervous and lacking in confidence. He desperately tried to please his owner and thought that if he went very fast and did everything super quick that this would please him. The first task we had to do was to explain to Gigalo that it was ok to be lazy. We spent at least a month just in walk, teaching

Gigalo to relax and slow his rhythm to his own natural tempo. We discovered that he had a real fear of being asked to work in an outline and his owner confirmed that he had been worked by previous owners in draw reins. The misuse of this equipment had caused Gigalo to be afraid of a contact and he would fight and pull against the hand as soon as he felt any pressure on his mouth. This made him run through the contact and things tended to go from bad to worse from there.

We taught Gigalo to look for lightness and how to give to pressure not fight it, we re-directed his bountiful energy into a more productive manner by channelling it upwards and inwards instead of forwards at 30mph! As he began to relax his confidence began to grow, this in turn allowed his owner to relax and for the first time they actually began to listen to each other. It was amazing how quickly Gigalo transferred his new found skills in walk into the trot and how his muscle structure changed as he carried himself correctly and in balance. This new found balance also instilled him with confidence and he began to show himself as the real dressage star we had always imagined. It was also interesting to note how his behaviour changed in his stable manners as his confidence grew. He was no longer bargy, he didn't mind staying in his stable overnight (apparently he was a real escape artist in other yards), he moved over when asked and was very respectful. Slowly and surely the really nice confident guy began to emerge and he softened in every way.

The big challenge came when we asked for canter. In previous instances he would take off as fast as he could and motorbike every corner. We had spent four months in walk and trot, teaching him to balance, bend and slow his rhythm, this would be a real test. With a deep breath and extreme self control, his owner asked him into canter by simply thinking the command and giving no visible aids. Gigalo picked up his canter rhythm from the same tempo as the trot and executed a perfect collected canter around the arena, bending in every corner and offering a smooth and light downward transition into trot as though he had been doing it all his life. It was a great success! At last he understood and at last his owner could trust him fully.

Gigalo continues to improve and has now forgotten his speedy past and looks every inch the super dressage horse he is destined to become.

NEVER SAY NEVER: Never Say Never was another interesting student. Again this chap and his owner arrived on our yard as liveries. A strapping 17.2hh chestnut he was the epitome of a giant scardy cat! Anything and everything was really, really scary and would elicit jumping to the side with manic snorting, eyes bulging and a heartbeat that could be heard 6ft away!

Riding Never Say Never was another challenge. A schooling session was a hard slog of fighting and kicking as his rider tried to bring him into an outline and keep him on the track. He would go very slowly then suddenly rush forwards making it very difficult for his rider to stay with him and in balance.

Initially all we needed to do with Never Say Never was give him a steady routine of stable management. Simply knowing what to expect and when, did wonders for his confidence and he slowly began to relax. Being turned out was a great help and living in a mixed herd in natural surroundings helped to channel his energies as he learned how to be a horse and how to think situations through logically (horsey logic of course). The difference in him in a few short weeks was astounding and the first lesson his owner took with us sealed the bond between them.

Never Say Never wanted very much to work in an outline, he just couldn't, simply because his owner was inadvertently blocking his every attempt to work correctly. A few small adjustments to the owner's riding allowed Never Say Never to instantly offer a beautiful shape with cadence and impulsion. His owner was delighted and they have continued to work together in this way.

The best example of how much Never Say Never has changed and grown as a bold individual came one day when his owner decided she would try some groundwork exercises with him. She decided that she would try to get him close to a white tarpaulin laid out on the ground. What helped Never Say Never that day more than anything else was that his owner's expectations were not high so no pressure was put on him to achieve a difficult goal. This allowed him the freedom to listen to his owner's gentle guidance and encouragement. He surprised us all by confidently approaching the tarpaulin and with very little prompting he not only walked across it but stood quite happily on it! For a horse that was frightened by his own shadow a few short months ago this was a huge achievement.

The knock on effect of this new found confidence is that Never Say Never's personality has had a chance to show through. He has a great sense of humour and is a real gentle giant, yes he still has his excited moments but this is nothing compared to the major traumas he had in the past. He very quickly settles down (within seconds) and regains his composure. May they continue to grow together.

SULLIVAN: I will always have a soft spot for a horse call Sullivan. When one of my clients sold on her horse she asked me to come with her to find a new youngster to bring on. We visited a very reputable dealer we knew and had a look at what he had in stock. Sullivan was standing in his stable a scraggy, gangly baby. All legs and innocence he looked like a little lost soul. We asked to see him out and moved around the school loose (Sullivan was unbacked) and, despite the fact that every leg faced a different direction when he stood still, he moved beautifully. My client decided to take him and I was given the task of backing him and helping their partnership develop.

Sullivan was such a nice, gentle chap. Willing and easy going (a bit cheeky like all little boys but with a heart of gold). He was very easy and straightforward to back and accepted everything we asked of him with an, "ok, if you say so" attitude. He was so good that we had to constantly hold ourselves back from pushing him too far too soon. It is a very easy mistake to make with willing youngsters and it doesn't take much to push them just that little too far and undo all of that open, honest work they have offered. Keeping ourselves in check wasn't easy but we knew that Sullivan needed time to mature mentally and physically. As he grew stronger and his muscle structure developed his legs straightened up and he began to grow into himself and slowly but surely an absolutely stunning individual appeared.

Within a year of backing him he went to his first show, tack and turnout. A nice class for a baby to learn all about the excitement of a showground. He took it in his stride, obviously thinking that everyone was there just to look at him! We continued to bring him on slowly, letting him get experience in showing classes and spacing out his competitions over the year. He didn't have perfect conformation but that was not important, he moved very well and he had great prescience in the ring.

The following year we felt he was mature enough mentally to cope with jumping. What Sullivan showed us was beyond our expectations. He had a natural flare for jumping, with huge scope and ability. We carefully nurtured this love and tried not to over tax him, giving him nice easy courses to bring his confidence to the fore. He combined his jumping ability with showing in working hunter classes and began to collect quite a number of rosettes.

Fortunately for Sullivan my client is a very experienced horsewoman and so would diligently work on exercises I gave her and report back her performance at shows. Every month or so we would get together and move Sullivan onto the next level until they were ready to go it alone.

My client has now begun to compete Sullivan in one day eventing and he is showing fantastic promise in this sport. She works away at his schooling and carefully manages his development, allowing him time to think and learn. Sullivan is rising 9yrs now and is beginning to mature into his eventing talent. Every so often my client asks me to help her through a problem or move him on that little bit further, and I feel a great deal of pride in their achievements and I am honoured to have played a small part in what promises to be a very long and fruitful partnership.

DUDLEY: Dudley was bought by his present owner around 3yrs ago. He arrived at his livery yard severely underweight and lethargic. His owner was a novice and this was her first horse but luckily for her she was stabling him on a very experienced natural horsemanship yard.

The first job was to get weight on him through careful feeding to build up his strength, but in doing so it was discovered that Dudley had an awful lot of energy and his owner realised that perhaps he wasn't the novice rider horse (schoolmaster) that he had been sold as. Dudley was quite simply manic and excitable and when his owner approached the dealer and questioned him on this now "wired" horse that was not the quiet ride she had been sold, his instructions were simply to starve the horse again and he wouldn't be so lively!

This was of course out of the question so steps were taken to re-educate him. Julie Irvine and Jo Fischbacher of Help4horses stepped up to the mark and  took great care in working with Dudley and his owner. Dudley was stabled at Julie's yard and as a result he was being handled everyday by very experienced people. He was very bargy on the ground, threw his head around and head butted anyone in his way, bucked under saddle and was all in all rather unpleasant to be around. Jo and Julie happily obliged his owner and took Dudley right back to basics. Careful correction and consistent handling on the ground helped re-educate him to the correct manners with humans and to build his confidence in himself and the humans around him. Under saddle however it was a different matter as he was prone to rearing and running off.

It became clear that there was more to his issues than had first met the eye. Further investigations were carried out and Dudley was examined by both physiotherapists and veterinary surgeons. It was discovered that the source of his issues lay in the fact that he had nerve problems in the coffin joint and this had a knock on affect on his shoulder, neck and back. The pain and discomfort that he felt on a day to day basis was almost unbearable but it was discovered that even though he was in great pain (and had been for quite some time) Dudley had been jumped by his previous owner whilst he was in this very uncomfortable and painful state. This had laid down a whole host of resentment and psychological problems.

It took around a year and half of consistent work and treatment by Jo and Julie to help bring this troubled boy to a state of mind and physical comfort that he could begin to rebuild his trust in people. Once Dudley discovered he had no physical pain he did not display the full range of behavioural issues that he had first come with. Some learned behaviour was present but overall his behaviour became manageable and Jo and Julie were finally in a position to begin to re-educate him.

I first met Dudley after all of the groundwork issues had been dealt with by Jo and Julie and Dudley's owner was starting to ride him again. His owner had trepidations (not without cause) and my task was to help her and Dudley re-build their trust in one another again. I visited Dudley at his yard on several occasions and continue to do so. In between my visits Jo and Julie continued with the schooling and teaching methods I  had put forward to help bring Dudley and his owner ever closer.

Dudley is an on-going case and still has a long journey ahead of him. However, he is a much happier boy and his owner is glad she stood by him and supported him through his dark times. His owner accepts now that Dudley will never be a novice ride and that this was an unfair task put upon him. However, his owner is rapidly becoming an experienced rider so in the not too distant future they will meet up on common ground! This in itself deserves high praise as there are few people who are willing to give up 3years of their riding time for a horse who had thrown them and shaken their confidence on numerous occasions. Now, because of this commitment by his owner, Dudley can at last repay her for all her love and dedication by trying his utmost best to be a good boy and be sensible at all times. (He still has his moments but he is trying very hard) Well done to his owner, she is an inspiration to us as she has proven that there are owners out there who are willing to take the time that is needed to help a troubled horse.

ALLY: Ally was backed by his owner and was a kind and willing little horse. However, Ally's owner was forced to sell him when he was seven and she never forgave herself, always wondering where he was and how he was getting on. Then, four years ago, she had the good fortune to be able to buy him back after seven years apart. What had happened to Ally in those years she will never know but he was a completely different horse to the one she had known and loved.

Ally was aggressive, anxious and stressed. He would bite if he was groomed and would kick out with both back legs if you approached him with tack. The worst thing his owner found was if you tried to approach him or another horse in the field, Ally would charge at you at full gallop, teeth bared and intent on driving you out of "his" space.

Fortunately though, his owner remembered the loving gentle little horse she had backed and knew that he was in there somewhere and that he had a reason for his behaviour. She had him checked by a physiotherapist and it was discovered that he had severe back problems, with a trapped sciatica nerve and muscle damage. This required lengthy and ongoing treatment to try to free the nerve and remove the pain. His owner did not ride him for two years and she had already decided that if needs be then she would retire him. She discovered that he had fallen in a trailer and the driver had continued on his journey with Ally hanging from the lead rope. He had been ridden every day (sometimes for several hours) with badly fitting tack and his damaged back. This meant that Ally began to hate the very concept of being ridden and people in general. He had probably tried to let people know he was in pain but no one was listening. He

was labelled dangerous and vicious and kept isolated from other horses. Fortunately from him is owner understood that it would take a long time to undo all the damage that had been done and that despite the fact that the pain had gone the memories of the pain were still there.

First of all his owner had to disassociate being caught and being groomed from being ridden and when she finally achieved this he began to transform. He stopped biting and being defensive, he never offered to kick and was easy to catch. His owner understands that she will never be able to remove all of his negative behaviour and that the damage has been done, but she can minimise his bad associations and slowly progress to finding the kind little horse she had once known.

The big challenge came when he was given the all clear by the physiotherapist and his owner started to bring him gently back into work on the ground. Ally progressed to a point where he was happy, relaxed and keen to do more, at this point his owner contacted me and we devised a programme to try to help him overcome his fear of the saddle. Using short sessions his owner used a bareback pad to let Ally understand that having a rider on his back did not mean the same kind of pain that had been caused by ill fitting tack. This gave him the time he needed to realize that it no longer hurt to be ridden. I worked with his owner on ridden exercises teaching Ally how to lift his back and open his shoulders without fear of pain. His short choppy stride (the Shetland pony had a bigger step!) slowly loosened off as he became more and

more confident. He began to work in an outline and cover the ground with an open fluid stride that hinted of the Arab genes he had mixed with his native blood. Eventually Ally's confidence had grown to a point where he could be ridden with a gulletless, treeless saddle and where he could be tacked up without any aggression or fearfulness. His work on the flat has improved immensely and his owner has almost got her old Ally back, the happy go lucky boy she had backed all those years ago.

Ally still has reservations about a normal saddle being put on his back (he definitely feels the difference between a gulleted and a non-gulleted saddle) but he is so safe and happy in his work now that his owner doesn't really mind if she never has a "real" saddle ever again.

How do horses suffer such breakdowns, how does it happen? I have talked about stress and the affects can have on a horse but recently an incident happened which highlighted most profoundly the knock on affects such stress can have.

The best natured of grooms or owners, when put under unreasonable pressure to perform in their jobs either through understaffing, inadequate equipment, long hours and poor facilities (although even the best of facilities can still put extreme pressure on people), can start to show mood swings and short tempers which often results in them taking out their frustrations on the horses in their charge.

It is all too easy for a stressed person to hit out with whatever is in their hands when pushed by a horse (who is often only being a horse). They may be sweeping up the yard, just one of a million things they have to do that day, and a horse is continuously kicking the door. This can wear on their already frayed nerves and as they pass the door they might swing the brush up and chase the horse off the door and into the back of the stable. Initially this may only be done as a threat but over time it becomes habit and the swing becomes a tap or dunt with the shaft of the brush, fork, shovel etc. Then it starts in the stable, the horse is dancing about as they are trying to muck out, kicking through piles of dung making it even harder for the groom to do his or her job, they smack the horse with whatever tool they have in their hands in total frustration, and so it may continue, till it is almost second nature to hit a horse soundly with brush shafts, fork handles or shovels, even grooming brushes can be used to hit a horse (especially a metal curry comb).

I witnessed just such an incident where a groom had got into a habit of jabbing horses on the quarters with a four pronged bulldog fork, albeit on their rugs, to move them around the stable. I warned her on numerous occasions that she would make a mistake one day and do this to a horse with no rugs, but as she was yard manager and I was a lowly groom at the time my warning fell on deaf ears. Then the inevitable happened. She was stressed out one day and not feeling well and one of her horses (who was supposed to stand on the concrete and not on the nicely banked straw) knocked down the banked straw as she tried to stand on the softer surface. The girl's temper broke and she struck out in anger, stabbing the horse twice on the quarters with the fork. The horse had no rug on for protection and suffered two sets of four puncture wounds to her quarters the wounds were deep and infected and required extensive medical treatment. The girl was sacked on the day and charged for animal cruelty.

Some of you may be shocked by this but there may also be some of you feeling a little bit shamefaced and guilty. I do not condone the girls actions one bit, but I know how easy it is to hit out in anger when you are pushed to the very limits of endurance. I have personally witnessed (in my younger years as a groom) a horse beaten with wooden pitchfork handle till he lay down in terror, unable to think of anything else to do. He was then punched and kicked till he got up. This was considered acceptable "discipline" behind closed doors, and may I add that both of these horses were full livery clients and the owners had entrusted the facilities with their care and welfare.

I know for a fact that this still goes on, even though it is illegal, and those responsible should know better. I can usually tell when a horse has been beaten, in my line of work I try to fix the trauma such treatment causes. Often a horse will be openly defensive and aggressive or nervous and afraid, but sometimes even I miss the small give-away signs that a deeply traumatised animal will show.

Often the effects of such treatment do not surface for many years and often it is the innocent bystander or kind owner who suffers the consequences. There are some types of horses, usually genuine characters who wish only to get along with people who suffer such abuse and, not wishing to harm anyone, will shut down and withdraw into themselves, trying to be as stoic as possible and hoping that if they just remain frozen then everything will go away. We met just such a character recently.

A client of mine was on the lookout for a schoolmaster for easy light schooling and hacking only. We saw a potentially perfect candidate advertised and duly went out to see him. My client had spoken at great length with the owner and was open and honest about her riding ability and the fact that she had a hip replacement and required a really steady and reliable character who would be quite happy plodding around.

We went to see the horse and he was a really nice guy. He was an older horse quiet and well mannered and although he had badly scarred legs he came forward with a genuine politeness and trying nature. There were little things that I did not pick up on at the time, such as he was not put into a stable but cross tied in a wash bay to be groomed. Granted there are some yards where this is standard practise and I assumed this was one. I was horrified at the tack that was put on him and the saddle was such a bad fit that I asked for another to be brought out. The girl was obliging and we found one that fitted a little better but still not well. I rode the horse and he was perfect, a real tryer, despite the fact that the tack obviously did not fit and must have been hurting him he did his best for me in all three paces without any resistance. My client rode him and was equally delighted. We decided to take him.

On arrival we noticed straight away his "shut" down stance in the stable. He would not even eat his hard feed or hay if anyone was in the box with him. It took him several days to be confident enough to nibble his hay as he was groomed and tacked up. The real indication that he was a troubled horse came when the maintenance manager was sweeping the yard past his stable and he became very frightened and ran back into the stable snorting. We knew then that he had suffered abuse. Over the course of the next few weeks the little signs were beginning to point quite clearly to the fact that at one time or another he had been beaten with yard tools. This also manifested in ridden work. Despite being assured that the horse was "fantastic at the beach" when the owner took him down to the river the horse was so afraid that he panicked and unseated the rider and ran back to the stables (bearing in mind that this rider is a lady with a hip replacement who was looking for a schoolmaster!) Full marks to the owner for persevering with the horse and in his defence he was a gentleman in the school and on hacks (unless you took him near water!).

The grand finale came when he took a panic attack in the stable (this is where we figured out he had been beaten specifically around the head and front legs). I went in to skip him out with a fork and skip bucket, the same way I had been doing for weeks, and this time he was standing in such a way that the only way I could get in and past him was to duck under his head. He had been wary of the tools but had coped up until now if you moved quietly and carefully and kept passive and stayed around his quarters when working and he would move willingly out of your way. He moved away from me in fear, making it impossible to duck under his head, so I took the opportunity to do a little advance and retreat to help him understand he did not need to be afraid. I followed him around until he stopped moving then I stopped and just as I was about to back away and take the pressure off he panicked and swung towards me, trying to get his head to the other side of me. Unfortunately for me (and him) he didn't lift his head high enough and clunked me quite severely on my head (didn't knock any sense into me of course). I simply remained quiet and shrugged my shoulders, brushing it off as just one of those things as the horse stood at the far end of the stable shaking with fear and waiting for the inevitable beating. I simply started to muck out then noticed something odd, I looked at the blood pouring onto the shavings in total confusion for a moment before I realised that it was me that was bleeding. The horse had been in such a panic that he had split my head open in his desperation to get away from the fork, purely bad luck. So, eight stitches later (and none the wiser!) we discussed with the owner the best course of action.

It was a genuine mistake on the horse's part and he is such a great guy that we both agreed that although he is clearly a remedial horse with a lot of hang ups that need to be addressed and not the quiet schoolmaster that he was advertised as, he is worth the effort in trying to help.

I explained to the owner the type of abuse he clearly must have suffered and explained that often abused horses (like humans) go through different stages of recovery. It is clear now that he had been shut down and had withdrawn from the world due to his handling and his fear of the punishment that was regularly meted out to him. This type of horse, when handled with sensitivity and care, can react in several ways. They can begin to try to ask for help by showing what they are afraid of (like this horse) but sometimes they almost try to goad or provoke a reaction from the handler in order to illicit the abuse they have been used to. This is almost like a "victim" syndrome. They may be so conditioned to abuse that they cannot cope with or deal with being handled in any other way and will behave in a manner that would normally cause them to be physically punished. Sometimes this type of horse will eventually come round and begin to respond to kind handling and begin to regain their confidence and trust in people again, however, sometimes they cannot and in this instance it is kinder for the horse to be put to sleep.

It is a huge responsibility for the new owner to decide the best course of action. Fortunately for the horse and his new owner, they are stabled on my yard and I feel that this horse is such a genuine character that he can come through this successfully. The owner knows that the journey may be a long one and that it may get worse before it gets better but we are all willing to give the horse the chance to be himself again, with no fear and not shut down, only time will tell.

So, the knock on affect of that simple break of temper by a groom or owner, that simple action can start a chain reaction that may go on for years, building in the horse until it is finally released, often with devastating affects. Like a stone thrown into the pond, our actions create ripples that fan out over time. Positive actions create positive ripples that strengthen the bond between human and horse. Negative actions create negative ripples that serve only to destroy such bonds and drive our species apart. What ripples do your actions send?

It is said that to be truly horsy you must have horse blood in your veins. For any horseperson the need to be with horses is almost all consuming, it is a drive, an obsession, a need. I want you all now to stop for a minute and look back on your life so far (some of us may need a telescope for this!!) and try to remember what it was that burned in you to make you love horses.

For most of us the obsession has been with us forever, from our earliest memories we seemed to be drawn to pictures, toys, stories etc about horses. We would play games where we were the horse or we were riding our majestic steed around our rooms or our gardens. We would gaze in wonder at the paintings of Unicorns or Pegasus seeing the mystery, wisdom and deep magic that the equine breed has upon humans. The love of the nobility, grace and gentleness of the horse cast a deep spell over us and we would wish with all our hearts that we be honoured with the companionship of a real live equine friend, our own special link with the magic contained in their deep, wise eyes.

For some of us the wish was granted sooner rather than later, we were the lucky ones who managed to go to riding school, or even have their own pony. Try to remember what it felt like when you saw a real horse in front of you for the first time. How privileged you felt you were when they turned their great heads and allowed you to gently pat their soft nose or if they blew sweet breath into your face. You knew then that this was the best feeling in the world and one which you wanted always.

As a child especially it seemed like magic and the love and respect you had in your hearts for these majestic animals was often reflected back to you. It is sad then that it did not always remain this way.

Most of us won't remember exactly when the shining light became tarnished; often things crept up on us a little bit at a time. Being older does not necessarily mean you are wiser, yet we would find ourselves in the company of more experienced people who did not seem to see their horses in the same way as you. The noble, magical creature that we had felt honoured to just be near slowly started to be just an ordinary, dull, animal, one who had to be told what to do and dominated at every opportunity. "Don't let him away with that!" "Tell him who is boss!" became the war cries and when we looked at our horse the eyes that looked back were often closed and sad. For many of us the loss of this special connection made us harden our hearts. We concentrated on "doing" things to or with our horses rather than "listening" to them. We may have progressed as good riders, even reaching high levels in competition or we simply may have continued to go to riding schools or became teachers ourselves. For most though there was always a feeling that something had been lost and the gap was often filled by resentment, ironically enough, towards the horses we worked with.

We may have found ourselves looking at our horses as objects, things to be used and discarded when no longer suitable or "broken". They may have become a means to an end, we would be angry with them if they did not live up to our expectations and when they did their best we took it for granted, expecting them to be great in gratitude for us owning them. For some of us many different horses may have passed through our ownership and all we would see is the physical ability the horse had to allow us to win rosettes or gain prestige. If we met children or adults new to the horse world we would feel it our moral duty to "educate" them to reality. After all, we have many years of experience to share, we knew how difficult and dangerous horses could be, how they could hurt you and how they could not be trusted. We would "help" the new people understand the truth and show them how to get results. We would be pleased when we saw our words of wisdom taken on board and the new owner conforming to our way of doing things.

Some of us however, manage to get a second chance. If you have ever watched a horse with a very young or disabled child, you will see that spark of magic once again. The openness of the child is reflected by the horse and they connect in a way that many of us have forgotten. The biggest horse will allow the smallest child to pull their whiskers or eyelids or sit on their backs and the care taken by the horse over their small charges is commendable. The love exchanged between child and horse is unspoken and total trust. We demand that our horses be honest and trust us, how many of us are able to be honest and trust our horses.

It may be that us "older and wiser" horse people should learn from the "newcomers". If you have ever seen a new owner or rider interacting with their horse and seen the absolute joy in their eyes just to be near the horse it is a special thing. They have what some of us have lost, the truth of why we have horses in the first place. We may have the knowledge gained over the years of the physical aspects of horse care etc but they still have the connection. It doesn't take much to regain that connection, just look at your horse as you would have as a child. The horse doesn't have much to gain from their relationship with us, they don't need to let us ride them, they don't need to obey us. I have seen horses who have been horribly mistreated by humans, but still they are trying to trust and be open, all the human has to do is open up to them. Wouldn't it be wonderful if we had never had our shining light tarnished, if we had kept the joy and gained the knowledge. It is not impossible, there are many gifted horsepeople out there with that special connection, the heart for the horse. They have either regained their love or have never been disillusioned.

There may be some who are happy to be what they are now. To be "the realist" to be "practical" and to be "getting on with the job" and that is fine, but don't expect everyone to be that way. The role of the horse and our relationship to the horse is changing, we are slowly becoming more "enlightened" and are seeking something more than a possession.

What I would say to you all is that it is a good thing to stop and think why you wanted to be with horses in the first place, to dominate, to gain prestige, to have a voiceless punch bag? Or perhaps it was for the love of such a graceful, noble creature with a wild heart that is willing to be a friend to us? It is not too late to regain the magic you saw as a child, just be open and respectful with that patient equine waiting for you outside.

Chapter Seven
What the Students Say

Tia the Friesien by Joanne Hull, author of Pet Psychic

When I first took Tia on, nearly 4 yrs ago, people thought I was mad. Here was this wild, completely unhandled, completely terrified 2yr old mare that would not let a human within a few feet of her, let alone touch her. She had been

born at her yard and no human had been able to touch her since, she did not have a bright future ahead of her as she was seen as a nuisance and a waste of space and things were looking very grim for her.

We herded her onto the trailer and took her on a journey that saved her life. I was able to keep Tia at home with me and my old Shire Toby. This was what Tia needed, time. I worked with her every day, slowly but surely building up her trust and letting her know that she would never be hurt or frightened again. Toby was a star and he helped her as much as I did. With his guidance and confidence I was finally able to touch her after almost a year of working with her every day. People still thought I would not get far with her because she was so wary of humans, but, over time we were able to handle her, brush her and lead her safely.

Two years later my circumstances changed and I had to work away from home a lot. I knew that I would have to put Tia, Toby and my friend's horse Jimmy on full livery somewhere and I really struggled to find a suitable yard. My biggest problem was Tia, I had taken so long to get her confident with people that it would be devastating for her if she was mishandled in any way. I was at my wits end when finally I saw and advert for Livery at Ross Dhu Equestrian, a yard owned by Morag Higgins. As soon as I walked onto the yard I knew that I had to have my horses here. Unfortunately Morag did not have three stables available, only one. I put my name on the list and prayed that we would move soon. In the meantime I put my three horses onto a yard that I hoped would care for them well. To trust a stranger with your precious horses is a very difficult thing and there are very few yards like Ross Dhu Equestrian, a yard run with the Equido ethos. Much to my dismay, my horses were very unhappy in their temporary yard, Tia was beginning to become nervous and withdrawn, Jimmy was neurotic and Toby was depressed. Then, after only a few short months, Morag called me and said they had built more stables and now had three available if I wanted them. I was delighted and moved my horses that day.

Tia was now rising 5yrs old and I knew she needed a job. The careful and patient handling by the Ross Dhu Equestrian Team had brought Tia back to the point where she was calm and manageable again. I was still travelling with my work and so was unable to spend much time with my charges, but I knew that they were all very safe and happy in their new home. Morag called me one day and asked if I wanted her and her team to "start" or "back" Tia. I would quite literally never have trusted anyone except the Equido Team to do this for me. I knew what Tia had went through in her short life and how much she trusted the staff at Ross Dhu Equestrian. I said yes and to my delight my beautiful Tia was a complete star. I had the privilege of watching her the day a rider sat on her for the first time and I was crying with pride. She was so happy and relaxed and proud to be working with humans. I can honestly say that I don't think any other yard could have achieved this with Tia and I was so delighted that I recorded the moments and you can see them on YouTube under Tia the Friesian's first day at school.

Equido ethos is unique and essential in today's world. The humanity and humility with which all the team work with their horses is overwhelming and I for one am so glad that we found the home we were looking for. I could trust no one else with my dear horses.

Finding My Horse - Liz Farquhar

My dream to own a horse nearly turned out to be a complete disaster if it wasn't for the help, support and encouragement of the Ross Dhu Equestrian Team. I purchased a handsome little 15hh coloured cob from an advert in an equestrian magazine. When I went to visit him I was told he was 5yrs old, but when we got him vetted and home it turned out he was barely 3yrs old. Casper had a lot of issues, not badness, but anxieties which we worked on together with the help of the Ross Dhu Equestrian Team. Using the Equido training really helped Casper and I learn to work together and for two years we progressed as far as we could. Casper was a very, very bouncy little boy with load of expression. I on the other hand, did not feel comfortable with his exuberant paces and he did try his best to be slow and smooth but just couldn't resist putting in the odd bouncy step which would throw my balance. So, after much soul searching I decided to find a new owner for Casper. The Equido Team stepped in and found a fantastic girl who was looking for her first horse. She and Casper were perfectly matched and she owns him to this day, frequently sending me updates and pictures of the fun the two are having with dressage, jumping etc. She cannot thank me enough for selling Casper to her and I am so happy that they have both found each other.

The search began for a new horse and I thought I had found the perfect boy in Orion, a very handsome grey TBX 16 hh. However, he turned out to have major psychological problems and was most definitely not the schoolmaster I was sold.

I could not ride him because he bucked, reared and bolted. I could not groom him because he would run away to stand shaking in the corner of his stable. If I approached him, he would turn away and face the wall. I was distraught.

I could sell him on and make him someone else's problem and try to recoup some or all of my money to buy another horse and, if I'm honest, these thoughts did go through my head, but, something was stopping me. It was his eyes.

When he looked at me with his sad expression, I felt his fear of humans. He wasn't threatening me - he was afraid of me. "What on earth has happened to you?" I asked him.

After much deliberation and discussion with the Equido Team the decision was made. He would not be sold on as I could not in conscience be responsible for, at best someone else's accident, at worst - well draw your own conclusion. We would work together, trying to build up his broken spirit and repair the damage that had been inflicted upon him by others. We set about our cunning plan to include lots of ground work, gentle but firm handling, and most importantly, consistency. Orion was given space to be himself. His field etiquette was impeccable and he soon rose in the herd pecking order to be one of the respected leaders.

As it transpired, retraining and learning was for us both. Orion was a true mud magnet and became the dirtiest grey on the planet. He was learning to be a horse again. He was at his happiest having so much fun playing and gal- lolloping about the field with his chums. I learned that having a clean horse was not as important as I thought - a happy horse is much better.

We both learned that grooming could be fun if done sparingly; allowing each other to accept that we both can make a mistake and it's OK. As such, we both learned patience. Working around such a sensitive horse who picks up on every emotion, my feelings, thoughts and even anxiety did not go unnoticed - Orion was my mirror.

I learned to make time and not rush things. It was a hard lesson but worth it. Orion became more secure and relaxed with me working around him and sometimes he would show the much needed affection and trust that we both craved. In summing up, he was on the mend. Eventually, after five months working together he was ready to move on to the next phase of his recuperation.

We found a sanctuary that would secure his future because we decided he could never be sold on. Orion would be a happy hacker with people who were experienced horsemen, fully aware of his issues, and who will continue the good work.

Now I am horseless with no finance to buy another to replace my Orion, but I'm content he can become the horse he was always meant to be.

I'm pleased to share with you that my story does have a happy ending for us both. Before I bought Casper, Morag Higgins had taken me and my husband to visit a young 3yr old she thought would be ideal for us. His name was Womble. We both loved him but I was always told not to buy the first horse you see. So we passed by and I purchased

Casper. About a year after buying Casper we were looking in the equine newspaper and saw Womble was for sale, his original owners had backed him and put him back on the market. We jumped at the chance and bought him for my husband Neil. The Equido Team schooled Womble for us and made sure he was a quiet safe ride for my husband and in between horses I was allowed to ride him too. Now that I no longer have a horse my husband and I have decided to share Womble and you know, Morag was absolutely right, he is the perfect horse for the both of us. I try to consol myself by thinking that without the help of the Equido Team Casper and Orion would not have had such a bright future and so I was fated to purchase them. It has been an expensive learning experience for me, but an invaluable one which has allowed me to learn and grow as a person and develop my own self confidence, a confidence which could so easily have been destroyed without the help and guidance of the Ross Dhu Equestrian Equido Team. Thank you all.

Jo Fischbacher

I have been around horses most of life but have always been uncomfortable with traditional training methods. I enrolled on the Equido course with little idea of how much it would change my life. Initially I thought it would help me improve my bond with my horse and help improve my

ability to train other horses. Equido has certainly done that, however, it has also completely changed my life.

I have suffered mental health issues all of my life and been on medication for many years. Equido teaches you a completely new way of thinking which is not just relevant to horses. For the first time in many years I have not been on medication and been the most mentally stable I have ever been. This has had a huge impact on relationships and my general well being. As for my bond with my horse, this has went to a level I didn't think possible. The impact on my horse's well being has been a huge transformation. He is the happiest and most relaxed horse compared to the anxious and occasionally aggressive horse he used to be. Equido is not just about training horses. It will take you and your horse to a level of communication you didn't believe possible.

Ross Pirie

Equido is a brilliant blend of horse care, psychology and good old fashioned common sense.

Having trained and worked in the horse industry for many years, I have learned and seen many things, I have come across many people's ideas about how you should work with

horses. I was always looking for something more with horses, a better connection without losing the grounded practicality. I have found this with Equido, it opened my eyes to a whole new world. I've learned the horses language and used it to help me work with them and help them in return. The level of horse care I have learned is of the top most knowledge and my discipline in riding has reached new heights.

Anybody looking for a natural view point in the horse world, enrolling on this course is a must!

David Watt

Hi there. A year ago I didn't know anything about horses. I've always seen them in fields but never thought I would be working with them and riding them.

I came to Ross Dhu Equestrian in 2009, I didn't know anything but I gave it my all. When I got close to the horse I was nervous, but as I kept learning Equido I learned how to speak their language. I have learned so much in a year, I can't believe it. I've learned how to approach them, handle them and how to use your energy.

If you are calm so is the horse, if you are hyper so is the horse. I learned about feeding and good horse care, it takes a lot to look after them.

So, thanks to Equido, I have learned so much and I would recommend it to anybody who would want to learn Natural Horsemanship the right way.

Maureen Martin

Having ridden my friend's horse which she kept at home (this bit of information is important!) I became, at the ripe old age of 53years, the very proud if somewhat fearful owner of my beautiful black shire-cross mare Hannah. The world of livery yards, owners, riding instructors horsey do's and don'ts rules and regulations came as a bit of a revelation to me and to be honest at times a somewhat unpleasant one.

"We've been on some pretty rum yards in our time "(and by the way these are Hannah's words through a horse whisperer not mine!) In those days although my equine knowledge was limited I knew that the way that some horses

were managed and trained was wrong. As lots of us have, I came across some horses which were badly even cruelly treated. However some were mismanaged with the best of intentions. I've known genuinely caring owners who have kept their precious charges stabled in winter" because the sky is dark and it will probably rain later". Horses are water proof for heavens sake and so are their rugs- or they should be! I also detested the attitude of" he /she will do as I say regardless. I'll show him /her who is boss" .As our Sunday yard manager at Ross Dhu says" We should listen to them. "There is nothing worse than a shut down horse. And so for the first few years of our time together Hannah and I moved around always looking for something better something different something that I knew would feel right.

I first met Morag at Ross Dhu almost five years ago. Hannah had had a particularly bad experience on a livery yard. She had become highly nervous and in fact quite dangerous. On the recommendation of my vet at the time (to whom I will always be eternally grateful) I searched for someone who would re-train her and I came across Morag and natural horsemanship. As it happened on that occasion we didn't come to Ross Dhu but she gave me loads of invaluable advice. I was also very impressed with the lay out of the yard.

I followed this visit by finding out as much as I could about Ross Dhu and the Equido system and we put ourselves on the waiting list. A couple of yards later and one year on I finally got the phone call "Do you still want to come? We have a stable for Hannah."

Since coming to Ross Dhu Hannah and I have come on in leaps and bounds. The Equido system allows horses to be horses. Morag Mark her husband and all the staff speak horse and the response from Hannah has been fantastic. She is allowed to live as naturally as possible she knows what is expected of her and she knows the boundaries. When it is appropriate the horses here are disciplined but in a way they can understand. They know no fear. I feel that it is also very important to note that although Mark has daily hands on experiences with the horses (I've never met anyone who speaks to them so quietly and calmly!) he also maintains the yard and land to the highest possible standards which in turn supports and enhances the Equido ethos. Some time ago one of our wonderful big horses died but Morag spoke to all the horses about him and helped them to come to terms with his death.

My riding has also improved since coming to Ross Dhu. Lessons are given to enhance confidence and guarantee success so both Hannah and I finish a lesson feeling good!

In conclusion Equido permeates the ethos here at Ross Dhu and Hannah has said (again through a horse whisperer) that she plans to stay!

Andria Reid

When Sophie and I arrived at Ross Dhu we were both taken aback by the peace and calm which surrounded the yard, it was a far cry to anything we had been used to. Sophie was my first horse and I had her for six years, in that time I had learnt so much from her and thankfully for me patience was one of her strengths. I was still unsure of myself though and the constant criticism we had both received over the years still made me doubt myself.

From being told that Sophie was too fat, I had been overhorsed, I looked awkward on Sophie, I must learn to get her on the bit more... etc.etc, it was hard to be confident. I had spent many hours in the school trying to tone Sophie and to get her on the bit. But I could never achieve this - why?? Perhaps all the critics were right. Of course with critics come supporters and I had a few of them too but there words were not as strong as the others. Through all of this I knew I one thing - I loved Sophie and would do anything for her.

After a few weeks at the yard I asked Morag for a lesson. The lesson was a key turning point in my relationship with Sophie, for the first time the lesson was about me. How to sit correctly, hold the reins and we started talking about the "energy" that Sophie would feel from me. I got Sophie to work on the bit as soon as I asked in the right way, she did not need a heavy hand (like some had suggested) , only to be asked properly. After that lesson I felt like I was floating on air and I am sure Sophie was delighted that at last I was listening to her. I understood that Sophie needed to build her strength up to work on the bit for a whole lesson, this was gradually built up.

However the most important thing was that my relationship with Sophie was so much stronger and the trust we have in each other is fantastic. I now think nothing of taking her out on my own and going for a gallop, this would have been unthinkable when I first arrived at Ross Dhu. We have even done a few endurance events, which again had helped build our bond. I know that it was Morag's style of training that made this difference and the encouragement that was given. I would never go back to the old style of being taught how to ride or improve, it just does not work for me. Equido recognises the horse has feelings too and that you must work with these. It is not about physical strength, it's about your energy - now if only I could apply this philosophy to other areas of my life then that would be truly amazing!

Thanks
Andria.

Susanne and Ralph

In the last couple of months, Ralph and I have moved to Ross Dhu Equestrian Centre. After many weeks of searching for a new yard and failing to find a livery that was of a high

 standard, I eventually found this professional, friendly and well managed yard. My horse was instantly made welcome and so was I. Everyone at the yard is so friendly and it makes it a really enjoyable place to spend your spare time. Most importantly though, the quality of care given to the horses by Morag, Mark and their team is first class. The horses come first and that was exactly what I was looking for. Before moving to Ross Dhu, my horse was an anxious individual but with the help of all at Ross Dhu, Ralph has become much happier and relaxed. Morag has a wealth of knowledge and expertise and weekly lessons with her have proved invaluable for both Ralph and I.

Thank you Morag, Mark and all at Ross Dhu.
Susanne MacCuish

Dawn Farquhar

After starting to study Equido I found that I began to learn more about how to help my horse understand what I was asking of him and in turn began to understand what he needed from me. I now feel that we both get more out of the time we spend together, whether it be grooming in the stable or going out for a ride.

After a very bad injury I lost all confidence and gave up riding. Equido helped me to remember why I love horses and how much they have to give. With the knowledge I've gained I now enjoy riding again, I feel safer as I've learned to listen to my horse and not just push him to do things that'll get us both hurt.

I found that learning how to work with your horse in a more natural way, you get a happier, healthier horse that is willing to give you everything you ask and more because you're asking in a way he understands

Chapter Eight
Words from the Horse's Heart
Poems by Mark Higgins

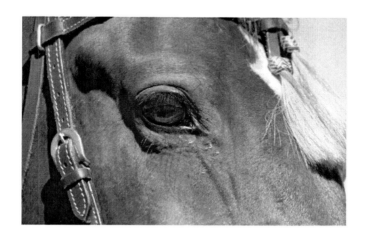

Notes for a new owner
Quiet my heart for I am lost.
Ease my soul from this darkened place.
Take my spirit from the pain I know,
Give back all that has been taken from me.

All I ask is for you to hear,
The voice that connects my soul to yours.
Gentle in its tone, soft in its touch,
Spoken the correct way we can achieve so much.

We go on from here.

Breath of life
Wind carry me on my way, breathe your life into me.
Never far away each day, whispering in the trees.

Cool my body as I gallop through the wild summer grass,
moving me ever forward until tomorrow's end.

As we dance throughout time,
Drawing ever on, both our spirits free, never to be tamed.

We are born in nature, free spirits wild as a storm,
Gentle as a summer's breeze, wind follow my heart

Wild heart
You will never tame my heart,
No matter what you say or shout
We will always be apart.

You can tie me up or tie me down,
And beat me to a pulp, I will fight you till my dying breath,
Where there is no air to gulp.

You will never understand me with those
cruel eyes of yours.
For you are blind to me and this will be your curse.

My language not of angry words or fist,
so subtle you can't see.
That whispered word or softest touch, this is the very key.

And so I will leave you now,
Inside your deepest darkest heart,
And wish someday to find that soul from whom I will never part.

Been it, seen it, done it
A poem from old wise horses

Been it, Seen it, Done it,
The old mares would say,
As they watched the youngsters frolic and play.

Old now, but young at heart,
In each other's company,
Never to part,

Until the time that greets us all,
When even warriors have to fall.

And to that place we all shall run,
Peace at last,
All battles won.

Been it, Seen it, Done it,
Nothing more needs said

Equiss

Soft eyes and an honest heart
Built for racing, not the cart.
Into our care a trusts been laid,
From times gone past a debt needs paid.

There's never been a place to meet
So many ego's to defeat.
But still they come down through the years
Their patient hearts to sooth our fears.

Because I know the thing they've found,
To give us a chance, some common ground,
They stand alone inside the pen
Offering us peace in this world of men.

They are equiss.

The empty stable
An empty stable is all we see through the tears.
No comfort found there for the passing of an old friend.

The bond has been broken
In Nature's way a tragic play of life and death, love and loss.

We know we have done what was right
But still it sits on us with its crushing weight.

Time will heal the wound in our soul
But our heart will always be broken when
We think of our old friend.

In memory of Piper

Sensei

My teacher doesn't talk to me the way that others do,
Sometimes I get down hearted for making him so blue.

I ask him "is this what your looking for" he simply
stands and stares,
How do I get into your mind to see what's going on in there.

And with that thought fresh in my mind, he lets a little slip,
Allowing me into his world and from his cup to sip.

Our different worlds collide in one all mighty flash
an ember glowing in my mind, a soul that burnt to ash.

For when the smoke has cleared it's there for me to see
A gift's been left behind, knowledge to set me free.

My teacher has four legs, a lovely mane and tail.
He has a world of knowledge but has no books to sell.

For when he lets you touch his heart, I think it's plain to see,
Your at the gates of heaven and he's given you the key.

Whispers

Mountian high, prairie wide, our lands are gone now,
no place to hide.

Our life with man, a tenuous link,
a beast of burden no right to think.

But still they come down through the years,
their gentle touch to ease our fears.

They are the ones who know the way,
their selfless hearts are why we stay.

And when I'm asked what did they say,
I simply whisper then walk away

Hope dreamer
I've lost all my fire, my spirit's gone black,
And I long for that day that the light will come back.
We've seen the dark times and lost all our hope,
Promises broken at the end of a rope.

And still I hold on to a dream that's inside,
for a world full of light and no reasons to hide.
And so with that thought still fresh in my mind,
I hear a soft voice so tender and kind.

For this is the light I have dreamed of so long,
To bathe in it's beauty, so gentle and warm.
Hold onto your dreams or they will never come true,
And look for the light that brings hope back to you.

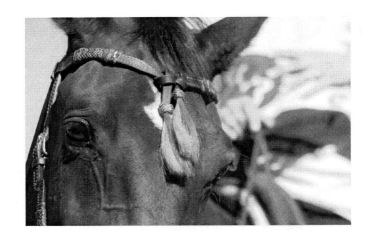

The horseman

Look for the small things
They are the key to it all
The slightest of pressure
However so small

The key's in your heart
Don't lock it away
Open the lock
Let the fear walk astray

And with this thought anew
Take hold of the reins
And peek through the curtain
To the world that you've gained

Blend with their movement
Like water form free
Give up your spirit
And just learn to be.

Your journey begins
At this point you start
At one with your horse
A long time to part

A gift has been given
From horsemen long gone
But its spirit live on
Like the words of a song

We thank the kind horseman
Both present and past
With a gift in their hands
Who's teaching will last

And so in the end
It's all down to you
For you to learn wisely
Or let the gift pass through

Home
Cold morning air on my face, good to feel
life's breath flowing through me,
Then I am gone, flying across the earth,
bathing in the morning sun as we dance
together,
No care or fear, just joy for the moment,
blending as one, our movements a ballet of
nature's making.

The herd settles, a mist covers our tracks and
the sun watches over us as we graze,
Content with it's warmth on our back
Horses surround me,
I am home